8.500 YEARS OF CIVILIZATION

GREECE

BETWEEN LEGEND AND HISTORY

editions HAÏTALIS

GREECE

CONTENTS

© Editions Haitalis

Editing and DTP: Barrage Ltd
Texts: Maria Mavromataki
Translation: Cox & Solman
Art Editing: Fotini Svarna
Colour seperations: Haitalis
Printing: Papadopoulos S.A.
Photographs: Haitalis
Publishing Co. archive

Published by: Haitalis
13, ASTROUS ST.,
13121 ATHENS, GREECE
Tel: 5766.883
Fax: 5729.985
www.haitalis.gr

PERIODS AND IMPORTANT LANDMARKS IN GREEK HISTORY

A

- THE PALAEOLITHIC PERIOD (Approx. 60000 - 8000 BC)

Human habitation in Macedonia, Epirus, Thessaly, Seidi cave in Boeotia, the Peloponnese, Euboea and the islands of Alonissos, Corfu and Cephalonia.

- THE MESOLITHIC PERIOD (8000 - 6500 BC)

This period is identified with the finds from Fragchthi cave near Ermionida in the Peloponnese, which included obsidian from the island of Melos, thus proving that trading by sea was taking place even in this very early period.

- THE NEOLITHIC PERIOD (6500 - 3000 BC)

Transition from hunting and gathering to the food-producing stage, with farming and stock-breeding activities (domestication of animals), the growth of the first permanent settlements, and the introduction of hand-made pottery. Numerous sites, throughout Greece. The period is subdivided into the Preceramic period (6500 - 6000 BC), the Early Neolithic (6000 - 5000 BC), the Middle Neolithic (5000 - 4000 BC, with Sesklo as a typical site, and the Late Neolithic (4000 - 3000 BC, with the Dimini settlement as a characteristic site).

- THE BRONZE AGE (3000 - 1100 BC)

p. 4

Vases of the Neolithic period from Dimini in Thessaly and Lianokladi near Lamia (National Archaeological Museum, Athens).

Below: a gold ring from Mycenae (National Archaeological Museum, Athens).

The use of metal (copper, silver, gold, lead) becomes general. Four major cultural units develop in and around the Aegean: the Helladic civilisation (mainland Greece), the Cycladic civilisation (the Cyclades islands), the Minoan civilisation (Crete) and the Trojan civilisation (north-west Asia Minor). The Bronze Age is subdivided into: the **Early Bronze Age** (3000 -

4

2000/1900 BC - Protohelladic, Protocycladic and Protominoan periods), the **Middle Bronze Age** (2000/1900 - c. 1550 BC, Middle Helladic, Middle Cycladic, Middle Minoan), and the **Late Bronze Age** (1550 - 1100 BC, Late Helladic or Mycenean, Late Cycladic, Late Minoan).

- 2000 BC: Arrival in what we call 'the Greek world' of the first Greek tribes.

-1900 BC: Founding of the first Minoan palaces.

- 1700 BC: Founding of the later Minoan palaces.

- 1550 BC: Establishment of grave circles A and B at Mycenae; the offerings found in royal burials indicate a sudden and mysterious accumulation of gold.

- 1500 BC: The volcano of Thera erupts, destroying the island.

- 1450-1400/1380 BC: Destruction of the Minoan palaces.

- 14th-13th centuries BC: Mycenean power extends to Crete, the Cyclades, the Dodecanese, Asia Minor, Syria, Palestine, Egypt, Lower Italy and Sicily.

- 1400 BC: Invention of Linear B, the first Greek script.

- 1350 BC: Founding of the first Mycenean palaces and fortresses.

- 13th century BC: Similarities between Mycenean centres in mainland Greece, the Cyclades, Crete and the East (Mycenean *koine*).

- 1200 BC: The Trojan War: destruction of the Mycenean sites.

- 1100 BC: Movements of population; invasion of the Dorians and Thessalians.

p. 5

Above: View of the palace of Knossos in Crete, and the wall-painting of the bull-leaping from the same palace (Herakleio Archaeological Museum).

Left: the wall-painting of the fisherman, from Akrotiri, Thera (National Archaeological Museum, Athens).

Below: a marble figurine of a harpist from the Cyclades (National Archaeological Museum, Athens).

THE GEOMETRIC PERIOD
(1100/1050 - 700 BC)

- 10th century BC: the three Greek tribes (Dorians, Ionians and Aeolians) move into the Peloponnese, the Aegean islands and the coast of Asia Minor (first period of colonisation).
- An enclosed agricultural economy, with the *oikos* ('house') as the nucleus for the production and distribution of products.
- The political system is based on the authority of the king, the council of elders and the assembly of warriors.
- 8th century BC: Emergence of independent city-states (the system of government most typical of ancient Greece).
- 9th/8th centuries BC: Adoption of the Phoenician alphabet and adaptation of it to the vowel and consonant sounds of Greek.
- 8th century BC: The Homeric epics, the *Iliad* and the *Odyssey*, take their basic shape.
- The Greeks gain an awarenes of their national identity through their shared language, their shared ancestors and their common religious beliefs (establishment of the Olympic pantheon of 12 gods, founding of the first Panhellenic sanctuaries and, in 776 BC, of the Olympic Games, the first Panhellenic athletic contest).

- **Art:** In Geometric pottery, the vases are decorated with linear and geometrical motifs. The first schematic depictions of animals and human figures appear little by little.
- No large-scale sculptures: small figurines in clay or bronze are the rule.
- No buildings of a monumental nature, and no clear typological distinctions between temples and houses.

p. 6
Earthenware vessels of the Geometric period (Nat.Archaeol. Museum, Athens).

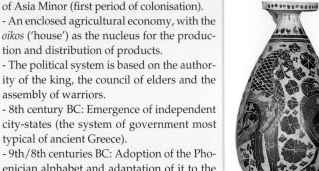

THE ARCHAIC PERIOD
(7TH - 6TH CENTURIES BC)

- 8th/7th century BC: The colonising activities of the Greeks become properly organised and cover the entire Mediterranean, as far as the Black Sea (second period of colonisation).
- Development of trade, shipping and industry. Greek ships rule the Aegean, displacing the Phoenicians.

- **Cultural changes:** The institution of monarchy declines, surviving chiefly in Epirus and Macedonia. Aristocratic (*aristoi* = landowners, nobles) regimes prevail, but tyrannical systems under by popular, powerful leaders are not uncommon. In 509/8 BC, Athens goes over to a democratic system of government, and democracy gradually spreads to other city-states.
- The foundations are laid for the organisation and development of the two most powerful Greek city-states, Sparta (aristocracy) and Athens (democracy).
- The minting of coins spreads throughout Greece soon after its invention by the Lydians in the 7th century BC.

- **Culture:** Development of poetic diction. Hesiod composes the *Theogony* and lyric poetry appears (Archilochus, Tyrtaeus, Terpander, Alcaeus, Sappho, Anacreon, Arion, Stesichorus). The Ionians (Thales of Miletus, Heraclitus of Ephesus, Pythagoras of Samos) lay the foundations of philosophy.

- **Art: Pottery**: In the 7th century, Eastern influences begin to have an impact on the decorative motifs of Greek pottery (the Orientalising period). The pottery of Corinth is predominant in the Greek world. The Corinthians invent the black-figure order, in which the figures and decorative motifs are in black paint which contrasts with the light-coloured background. The potters of Attica take over and develop the black-figure order, and during the 6th century BC surpass their colleagues in Corinth. Late in the sixth century, the red-figure order is invented in Athens: now the figures in the scene retain the reddish colour of the clay and the ground is painted black.

Sculpture: sculptured works of greater height and mass come to be produced, and sculptors strive to organise them around their vertical and horizontal axes. The 7th century is called the 'Daedalic period', and it marks the beginning of the monumental Greek plastic arts. The *kouros* type (an upright nude male figure) and the *kore* type (an upright clothed female figure) become established during the 6th century.
The principal features of the age are the so-called 'Archaic smile' and the latent movement of the statues; greater naturalism is gradually introduced.

Architecture: the first monumental stone temples are built. In the late 7th century, the two orders of Greek architecture appear: the Doric order prevails in mainland Greece and the Greek colonies of the West, and is notable for its severity and plainness, while the Ionic order is encountered chiefly in Asia Minor and the Cyclades, its principal features being delicacy of form and an inclination towards ornamentation.

THE CLASSICAL PERIOD
(5TH - 4TH CENTURIES BC)

- 499 BC: The Greek cities of Ionia rise in rebellion against the Persians, to whom they became subject before the end of the 6th century. They receive assistance from Athens and Eretria.
- 494 BC: Miletus is captured and destroyed by the Persians; failure of the Ionian Rebellion.
- 490 BC: Darius, King of Persia, and his generals Datis and Artaphernes subdue the Cyclades, sack Eretria and are ultimately defeated by Athens and Plataeae at the Battle of Marathon.
- 490-480 BC: Thanks to the initiatives of Themistocles, its military commander, Athens becomes a naval power.
- 481 BC: A Panhellenic conference is held at the Isthmus of Corinth, and the assembled Greeks decide to combine to face the Persian threat.
- 480 BC: Xerxes, King of Persia, invades Thrace, Macedonia and Thessaly. The Battle of Thermopylae. The sea-battle of Cape Artemisium, Euboea. Athens is looted; the Greeks are victorious at the Battle of Salamis.
- 479 BC: Athens captured for a second time. The Greeks win again at the Battle of Plataeae, and finally vanquish the Persians at Cape Mycale, on the mainland opposite Samos.
- 478/7 BC: Founding of the 1st Athenian (or Delian) League. Athens becomes the leading Greek naval power, provoking the displeasure of Sparta.
- 461-445 BC: The 1st Peloponnesian War: initial clashes between Athens and Sparta, in which other Greek city-states (Argos, Thebes, Boeotia, etc.) become embroiled.
- 448 BC: Athens makes peace with Persia (the Peace of Callias).
- 445 BC: Athens and Sparta sign a thirty-year peace treaty.
- 461-431 BC: Athens reaches the zenith of its glory under Pericles (the so-called 'Golden Age').
- 432-404 BC: The Peloponnesian War, which sees the entire Greek world divided into two armed camps headed by Athens and Sparta. The Athenian alliance includes the Ionian cities of Asia Minor, the islands of the Aegean with

*p. 7
Marble statues of a kore (Acropolis Museum) and a kouros (National Archaeological Museum, Athens) of the Archaic period.*

the exception of Melos, the coastal cities of Thrace and Macedonia, Thessaly, Plataeae, Naupactus, Acarnania and the islands of the Ionian Sea with the exception of Leucas. Sparta's alliance brings together the city-states of the Peloponnese (with the exception of Argos and Achaea), Megara, Boeotia (apart from Plataeae), Phocis, Locris, Ambracia and Leucas.

- 405-404 BC: Athens is finally defeated when the Spartans are victorious in the Battle of Aegospotamoi on the Hellespont. Sparta, aided by Persia, drives out the democratic parties from the Greek city-states and installs oligarchic regimes.

- 395-386 BC: The Corinthian or Boeotian War, with a league consisting of Thebes, Athens, Corinth and Argos against the power of Sparta. The latter, with the help of Persia, imposes the 'Peace of Antalcidas' (386 BC), by which numerous Greek cities come under the sovereignty of the Persian king.

- 378/7 BC: The Second Athenian League is founded, and lasts until 355 BC.

- 371 BC: Clash between Sparta and Thebes at Leuctra. The victory won by Epaminondas of Thebes marks the beginning of the political ascendancy of his city-state.

- 370 BC: Epaminondas manages to form alliances with the Arcadians and the Messenians, founding the cities of Megalopolis in Arcadia and Messene in Messenia to serve as bulwarks against Spartan expansion.

- 362 BC: Battle of Mantineia, at which Epaminondas is defeated by the Spartans and killed. End of the period of Theban hegemony.

- 359 BC: Philip II, King of Macedon, expands his state until it becomes one of the strongest in the Greek world.

- 338 BC: Battle of Chaeronia, at which Philip defeats Athens and Thebes.

- 337 BC: A conference of the Greek city-states, meeting at Corinth, proclaims Philip general commander, emperor and leader of the campaign to be fought against the Persians.

- 336 BC: Assassination of Philip II. His son, Alexander III (the Great) is crowned king of Macedon. He captures and destroys Thebes. At Corinth, he is acknowledged leader of the Greeks and succeeds his father as commander of the Persian campaign.

- 334-323 BC: Campaigns of Alexander the Great.

- **Culture**: During the Classical period, philosophy reaches heights never achieved before and rarely since. Democritus of Abdera states the atomic theory; Socrates engages in his quest for truth and virtue; Plato founds the Academy in Athens and forms his theory of ideas; and Aristotle, of Stagira in Macedonia, sets up a school of his own in Athens (the Peripatus) and lays the foundations of logic and scientific research. Among the leading scientific personalities is the physician Hippocrates of Cos. In historiography, immortal works are composed by Herodotus, Thucydides and Xenophon. Verbal skills are cultivated by the Sophists and by important orators such as Lysias, Isaeus, Isocrates and Demosthenes. Choral poetry develops early in the fifth century, with Pindar of Thebes as its principal representative, and dramatic poetry, stemming from the nucleus of the cult songs in honour of Dionysus, begins to take shape as early as the late sixth century BC. The foundations of the theatre were thus

laid, and in the fifth century that art-form reaches its supreme pinnacle in the works of Aeschylus, Sophocles, Euripides and Aristophanes.

In **sculpture**, the early fifth century sees the introduction of the severe style, with the pediments of the temple of Zeus at Olympis as good examples. During the fifth century, the plastic arts succeed in finding the answers to the ques-

p. 9

Pottery of the
Classical period.

- **Art:** In **pottery**, the red-figure order develops and grows closer to the art of painting. The production of vases with a white ground flourishes, the white *lecythus* being a characteristic type. Painting makes great progress: among the best-known artists of the day are Polygnotus, Micon, Zeuxis, Parassius and Apelles. The wall-paintings in Macedonian tombs give some idea of what the art of the period was like.

tions posed by artists throughout history and in creating works of unique value thanks to their idealised forms, balanced proportions and harmonious masses. The sculptures executed by Phidias for the Acropolis of Athens are the culminating triumphs, though notable work is also done by Polyclitus, Alcamenes and Agoracritus, the last of whom bears a closer relationship to the elaborate style which comes in late in the fifth century BC. In the fourth century BC, sculpture tends to use movement to express inner concerns and the anguish of the spirit. The works of Praxiteles, Scopas, Lysippus and Cephisodotus stand out in this period.

In **architecture**, the Doric order reaches its final form in the temple of Zeus at Olympia (457 BC). There is much building activity, whose results are plainest in Athens, where elements from the Doric and Ionic orders are blended into a harmonious whole. The Parthenon on the Acropolis in Athens is a landmark in the achievements made by architecture in this period, attaining overall harmony in the union of opposites. After the works of the Acropolis, the construction of buildings of a generally secular nature becomes more general. First appearance of the Corinthian order.

p. 8

The Parthenon, on the Acropolis of Athens.

p. 9

Part of the Ionic east frieze of the Parthenon: Poseidon, Apollo and Artemis (Acropolis Museum).

THE HELLENISTIC PERIOD (3RD - 2ND CENTURIES BC)

- After the death of Alexander the Great, his empire shatters into fragments and gradually crystallises into five different kingdoms: those of the Antigonids in Macedonia, of Thrace, of the Seleucids in Syria, of the Ptolemies in Egypt and of the Attalids in Pergamum.
- 296 BC: Pyrrhus comes to the throne of Epirus, and unsuccessfully lays claim to power in Macedon. He dies in 272 BC.
- In mainland Greece, two important alliances emerge: those of Aetolia (Aetolians, Locrians, Dorians, Dolopians and some of the Acarnanians) and Achaea (many of the city-states of the Peloponnese). Athens and Sparta continue to be dependent on Macedonian policy. Rhodes and Delos emerge as important commercial centres, but the position of the Greek city-states weakens as a result of constant friction and fighting.
- 279 BC: The Gauls raid Greek territory.
- The threat of Rome first appears; 179 BC: defeat of the Macedonian king; 168 BC: Perseus, King of Macedon, is beaten by Aemilius Paulus at Pydna and Macedon becomes a Roman province; 147 BC: the Achaean League is defeated by Roman forces at Scarpheia in Locris, and Central Greece comes under the control of Rome; 146 BC: the Roman consul Mommius defeats the Achaeans again, at Leucopetra near the Isthmus of Corinth, and then sacks Corinth itself. This battle marks the final subjugation of all Greece to Rome.
- **Culture**: The philosophy of the period focuses on human life. Zeno founds the Stoic School, and Epicurus the school which took his name. Science continues to make rapid progress. Polybius is the leading historiographer. In the theatre, comedy reigns supreme (with Menander and Mimus as the representatives of the New Comedy).

- The **art** of the Hellenistic period revolves around the main axes of the aesthetic achievement and the 'theatrical' impression. The secular side of life is emphasised, along with the value of the human individual. In architecture, too, secular buildings are the rule, the Corinthian order spreads, and ornamentation is highly elaborate. Sculpture stresses the magnitude of human emotions through intensity of movement and expression. Progress is made in painting and the art of the mosaic (houses on Delos, at Pella, and elsewhere).

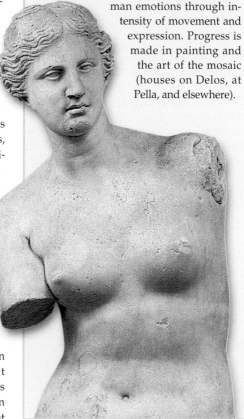

THE ROMAN PERIOD
(2ND CENTURY BC - 4TH CENTURY AD)

- 87/85 BC: The Greeks ally themselves with Mithridates, King of Pont, in a war against the Romans. 86 BC: Athens is wrecked and looted by the Roman general Sulla.
- 48-30 BC: Greece becomes a theatre of operations during the Roman civil wars (battles of Pharsala, 48 BC, Philippi 42 BC, Actium 31 BC).
- 27 BC: Octavian Augustus divides Greece into two senatorial provinces, Macedon and Achaea.
- 37 AD: Caligula robs Greece of many of its art treasures.
- 49-58 AD: St Paul travels in Greece spreading Christianity.
- 54-68 AD: Under the Emperor Nero, the sites of Delphi, Olympia and elsewhere are looted.
- 121-134 AD: The Emperor Hadrian visits Athens and other Greek cities, endowing them richly.
- 3rd century AD: Greece is ravaged by invasions of Goths.

- **Culture**: Greek civilisation has a marked impact on the Roman conquerors. Roman art, philosophy and literature are largely based on the achievements of Greek antiquity. Many of the emperors visit Greece, and are especially attracted to Athens, which becomes one of the Empire's most important centres of learning.

p. 10
Above: mosaic floor from Delos showing Dionysus on the back of a panther.
Below: the marble statue of Aphrodite from Melos (the 'Venus di Milo', the Louvre).
p. 11
The Roman theatre of Herodes Atticus in Athens.
The Arch of Hadrian in Athens (painting in the Vouros-Eftaxias Museum).

THE BYZANTINE PERIOD
(4TH CENTURY AD - 1453)

- 330: The capital of the Roman Empire is moved to Constantinople.
- 393: Theodosius I bans the pagan cults and abolishes the Olympic Games.
- 395: The Empire is split into eastern and western sections, with Greece becoming part of the Eastern Empire.
- 441: Greece is raided by the Huns.
- 529: Justinian closes the schools of philosophy.
- 7th-9th centuries: The Slavs spread out through Greece, reaching the Peloponnese and the Aegean islands. They are soon assimilated into the indigenous population and Hellenised.
- 726: Publication of the Byzantine decree banning the veneration of icons.
- 824: Crete taken by the Saracens.
- 842: Restoration of the veneration of icons.
- 961: Crete retaken by Nicephorus Phocas for Byzantium.
- 10th century: Formation of a Bulgarian state with expansionist designs.
- 1018: Bulgaria subdued by Basil II, 'the Bulgar-Slayer'.
- 1096: 1st Crusade.
- 1124-1126: The Ionian islands are looted by Venetians. Destruction of Methone; occupation of Cephalonia.
- 1147: 2nd Crusade.
- 1189: 3rd Crusade.

- Early 13th century: Venetian rule in Crete, Cythera and the south Peloponnese.
- 1204: 4th Crusade. Constantinople falls to the 'Franks' (Crusaders).
- 1204-1261: The Venetians occupy the Ionian islands, most of the Aegean islands, Crete, Euboea and trade-stations in the Peloponnese and Thrace. Adventurers from Western Europe rule mainland Greece, setting up the Kingdom of Thessaloniki, the Duchy of Athens and the Principality of Achaea.
- Resistance to the incursors from the West centres on the rump (Byzantine) Empire of Nicea (controlling Asia Minor, Thrace and part of Macedonia) and on the Despotate of Epirus, founded by Michael Comnenus Angelus Ducas (with its capital at Arta). Theodore Angelus, successor to Michael, extends his power into Macedonia and recaptures Thessaloniki in 1224.
- 1261: Constantinople is recaptured for Byzantium by the Emperor Michael Palaeologus VIII.
- 1262: The 'Franks' surrender to Byzantium the fortresses of Maina, Mystras, Monemvasia and Yeraki in the Peloponnese. The Frankish Principality of Achaea gradually withers away, and the Despotate of the Morea, with Mystras as its capital, is founded (1348-1460).
- 14th-15th centuries: The Greek world splits up into petty states which are constantly at war with one another. Byzantium is threatened by the Turks.

p. 12
The church of Our Lady Queen of All at Mystras, fifteenth century.

Byzantine art

- The Christian church is the most important creation of Byzantine architecture:

In the Early Christian period (330-7th century AD), the type of church called the basilica takes shape (numerous examples in Thessaloniki, Amphipolis, Philippi, Nicopolis, Athens and elsewhere). Buildings arranged symmetrically around their centre (circular, hexagonal and octagonal structures, others with four apses or cross-shaped) are also common.

In the Early Byzantine period (7th century - 843), the domed basilica type (church of the Holy Wisdom, Thessaloniki) predominates.

In the Middle Byzantine period (843-1204), the domed cross-in-square church prevails and this type spreads throughout Greece. The Middle Byzantine octagonal church is another common type. Much building is done in this period, and monuments from it can be seen all over Greece.

The Late Byzantine period (1204-1453) repeats the typological categories of earlier times, though the so-called composite type makes its appearance (Mystras), along with the raised transept type (Epirus, Euboea, the Peloponnese).

p. 13

Above: mosaic of Christ Pantocrator from the dome of Dafni Monastery, 1100 AD.

Below: Our Lady and Christ, a mosaic icon from Bithynia, fourteenth century (Byzantine Museum, Athens).

Byzantine painting can be studied in the wall-paintings, mosaics and portable icons which adorn churches even today. In the Early Christian period, mosaics are used on the floors and walls of churches, and are of a largely symbolic nature, often retaining elements from the Hellenistic tradition together with trends from the art of the East. The churches of Thessaloniki preserve some superb examples of such mosaics. During the period of the Iconoclastic Controversy, many figurative scenes are destroyed and replaced by non-figurative compositions. After the restoration of the veneration of icons, in 843, a new iconographic programme for churches develops, one which stresses the concept of Incarnation. The walls of churches are ornamented with scenes from the life of Christ (the Twelve Great Feasts) and with the figures of Christ Pantocrator, Our Lady, the Evangelists, the Apostles, and numerous saints. Under the Macedonian Emperors, an attempt is made to revive the Hellenistic tradition (the Macedonian Renaissance), while in the eleventh century the figures become entirely spiritual and transcendental. Under the Comnenus Emperors, emphasis switches to the expression of human passion. By the late twelfth century, three basic trends have become predominant in painting: the classical/monumental school, the elegant school and the dynamic school. There are outstanding examples of Middle Byzantine painting to be seen throughout Greece (Thessaloniki, Kastoria, the Monastery of the Blessed Loukas, Dafni, Naxos, Chios, Patmos and else

where). While the Empire is in 'Frankish' hands (1204-1261), the arts flourish in the Despotate of Epirus and in Thessaloniki. Under the Palaeologus Emperors (1261-1453), the so-called 'heavy' or 'massive' style gradually comes into fashion, leading - after 1300 - to a tendency to return to the classical models. Important wall-paintings of the Late Byzantine period have survived at Mystras, in the Protaton on Mt Athos, and in Arta, Thessaloniki and Verria.

TURKISH RULE
- THE MODERN PERIOD

<u>Note</u>: *After this point, Greek placenames and family names are usually rendered in phonetic transcription rather than in their Classically familiar forms.*

- The Turks conquer the Greek world piecemeal prior to the fall of Constantinople itself in 1453 (Thrace 1361, Thessaloniki 1430, Thebes 1435, the Peloponnese 1446). In 1456, they take Athens, in 1460 they overthrow the Despotate of the Morea, and by the late sixteenth century almost all Greece is in their hands. In 1669 Crete becomes theirs, too.

p. 14
Greeks in national costume on the monument of the Acropolis.

- 1463-1479: 1st Venetian-Turkish War.
- 1499-1503: 2nd Venetian-Turkish War.
-1684-1718: The Venetians gradually take control of the Peloponnese and parts of north-west Greece.

- **Eighteenth century:** First stirrings of rebellion among the Greeks, with the Orloff rising in the Peloponnese (1769-1770), the patriotic songs of Rigas Ferraios (1787), and the struggles for freedom of the Souliots of Epirus (1790-1803).

p. 15.
The statue of Theodoros Kolokotronis, a hero of the Greek War of Independence, in front of the Old Parliament in Athens (now the Historical Museum).

- 1797: Corfu taken by the French.
- 1800: Founding of the Septinsular Republic.
- 1809-1814: The Ionian Islands taken by the British.
- 1814: The Philiki Etairia ('Society of Friends') is founded to organise resistance activities against the Turks.
- 1821: Conventional year in which the Greek War of Independence begins.

- 1822: First National Assembly of the Greeks, at Epidaurus.
- 1823: Second National Assembly, at Astros.
- 1825: Siege of Mesolongi; 1826, the breakout of the besieged Greeks.
- 1826: National Assembly at Epidaurus.
- 1827: Third National Assembly, at Troizina; Battle of Navarino.
- 1828: Ioannis Capodistrias is elected as first Governor of Greece.
- 1829: Fourth National Assembly, at Argos.
- 1830: Greek independence.
- 1831: Capodistrias assassinated.
- 1833: Othon of Bavaria chosen as the first King of Greece.
- 1834: Athens becomes the capital of Greece.
- 1837: Foundation of the University of Athens.
- 1843: Revolution of 3 September; Greece granted its first Constitution.
- 1862: King Othon dethroned.
- 1864: Ionian Islands united with Greece.
- 1878: Cyprus occupied by Britain.
- 1881: Thessaly annexed.
- 1896: First Olympic Games of modern times held in Athens.
- 1897: Greek-Turkish War.
- 1912: Dodecanese occupied by Italy; First Balkan War.
- 1913: Second Balkan War.
- 1914-1918: First World War.
- 1922: Asia Minor Disaster.
- 1923: Treaty of Lausanne.
- 1924: Greece declared a republic.
- 1936: Dictatorship of Ioannis Metaxas.
- 1939: Outbreak of the Second World War.
- 1940: War between Greece and Italy.
- 1941: War between Greece and Germany.
- 1941-1944: German and Italian occupation, national resistance movement.
- 1948: Incorporation of the Dodecanese into Greece.
- 1952: Greece joins NATO.
- 1961: Association Agreement between Greece and the Common Market; full membership of the EC follows in 1981.
- 1967-1974: Colonels' dictatorship.
- 1974: Turkish invasion of Cyprus.
- Since 1974, the form of government in Greece has been parliamentary democracy under a president as head of state.

p. 16
The Tholos (fourth century BC) in the sanctuary of Athena Pronaea at Delphi.

p. 17
Characteristic landscapes in Greece.

CENTRAL GREECE

The region termed Central Greece is bordered on the north by Epirus and Thessaly (and is washed on the north-west by the Ambracian Gulf), on the west by the Ionian Sea, on the south by the Gulfs of Patra and Corinth and the Saronic Gulf, and on the east by the Aegean. The Malliakos and Euboean Gulfs lie between the east coast of Central Greece and the island of Euboea. Central Greece is a largely mountainous area, whose main ranges are as follows: Tymfristos (2315 m.), Panaitoliko (1924 m.), Othrys (1728 m.), Vardousia (2349 m.), Giona (2510 m.), Parnassus (2457 m.), Oiti (2153 m.), Kallidromo (1399 m.), Elikonas (1748 m.) and Kithaironas (1408 m.). To the south-west of Mt Parnassus lies the town of Amfissa, surrounded by the largest plain in the region. The main rivers are the Spercheios, the Acheloos, the Evinos and the Mornos. Most of the lakes are concentrated in the west of the region (Lakes Trichonida, Lysimachia, Ozeros and Amvrakia), with Lakes Iliki and Paralimni to the east.

ATHENS

A thens, which lies in the basin of Attica between Mts Parnes, Penteli and Hymettus, on the shores of the Saronic Gulf, is today the capital of Greece and the country's largest city. Its vital geographical position and the mild climate were the basic reasons why it was chosen for human habitation at a very early date. During its long history, the brilliant cultural achievements of Athens made an invaluable contribution to the human heritage.

PREHISTORY

The human habitation of Athens began to take on organised form as far back as the Neolithic Age, around 4000-3000 BC, when settlements were established on the rock of the Acropolis (near the north slopes), in the vicinity of the Ilissus River (where the temple of Olympian Zeus now stands), and in the area later occupied by the Agora. The human presence was uninterrupted throughout the Bronze Age, and in Mycenean times (1550-1050 BC) there was an important town on the Acropolis. Excavations have shown that early in the thirteenth century BC the **palace of the Mycenean king** was erected on five flat spots on the Sacred Rock. In the middle of the same century, the Acropolis was walled for the first time, with a structure later known as the **Pelasgian Wall**. At the same time, a secret water cistern was dug on the north-west side of the Acropolis, thus ensuring that the city would have a supply of water when besieged.

◄ *p. 20*
Above: view of the Acropolis of Athens.

Below: statue of Apollo in the Academy of Athens.

◄ *p. 21*
Statue of Athena in the Academy of Athens.

p. 22
View of the Acropolis: the sacred rock of ancient Athens still towers over the modern city.

The prestige of Mycenean Athens can be seen in the series of myths which are associated with the activities of local heroes. The first king of the city, in the myths, was Cecrops, while the most famous hero was Theseus, son of Aethra and Aegeus. It was Theseus who was said to have freed Athens from the cruel tribute of blood which the city was forced to pay to King Minos of Crete: every nine years, the Athenians were compelled to send seven youths and seven maidens to Crete to be devoured by the terrible monster called the Minotaur. Theseus killed the Minotaur and became king of Athens. The unification of the settlements of Attica under the leadership of Athens (the process known as *synoecismus*) was attributed to Theseus.

THE CLASSICAL PERIOD

The unification attributed to Theseus must actually have taken place quite a long time after the Mycenean period, in the eighth century BC, and it did much to boost the development of Athens. In the seventh century, the power that had previously been held by the kings passed into the hands of the aristocrats. In 624 BC, the laws of the city were codified for the first time, by Draco, and in 594 BC the Athenians commissioned Solon, one of the Seven Sages of antiquity, to compose a new code of laws. His innovations gave the system of government a democratic tone, in the sense that the offices which could be held by the citizens and the obligations to

which they were subject were determined in accordance with their income. In 561/560, Pisistratus established a tyranny in Athens - with the support of the broad mass of the people - and he and his sons Hippias and Hipparchus remained in power until 510 BC. In 508 BC, Athens acquired a fully democratic system of government under the reforms promoted by Cleisthenes. In the period from 490 to 480/479 BC, the Athenians led Greek resistance to the Persians in their attempt to expand their empire on to Greek soil. During the Persian wars, Athens was burned down twice, subsequently being reconstructed and fortified on the initiative of Themistocles. Themistocles was also the force behind the reinforcement of Athenian naval power and the setting up of what was called the Delian League, in 478 BC. This alliance, of which many Greek cities were members, had the primary objective of forming a common front to deal with the Persian threat, but Athens was able to use its leading position in the Delian League to become the most important city-state in Greece. In the political sphere, this period saw the rise of Pericles, the guiding spirit behind the 'Golden Age' which was the most brilliant period in the entire history of Athens.

In the time of Pericles, democracy reached perfection and all the sectors of intellectual life and the arts experienced moments of grandeur and glory. Nonetheless, even these achievements were not capable of preventing the

p. 23

The Panathenaic Stadium of Athens, constructed in marble. This was built on the ruins of the ancient Stadium to house the first Olympic Games of the modern times in 1896.

Peloponnesian War, which broke out in 431 BC and divided Greece into two armed camps, with Athens and Sparta as the principal belligerents. In 404 BC, Athens was finally defeated and embarked upon a slow process of decline. After an unsuccessful attempt to regain a position at the heart of Greek affairs by setting up a second League (in 379 BC), Athens was conquered by Philip II of Macedon in 338. Philip - and his son Alexander, 'the Great' - displayed respect for the city's cultural prestige, however. In the Hellenistic period, Athens was dependent on the policies of Alexander's successors, and in the second century BC passed into the Roman sphere of influence. In 86 BC, during the wars between Rome and King Mithridates of Pont, Athens was looted by the Roman consul Sulla, and it was many years before the damage was rectified. In the second century AD, the favours bestowed on the city by the Emperor Hadrian stimulated a late flowering of Athens, which grew out beyond the geographical boundaries of the past and acquired many fine new monuments.

Today, the monuments of Classical antiquity are scattered all across the city, but the supreme creations are the sacred buildings of the Acropolis. The **Acropolis** was the place in which the cult of Athena, the most important goddess in the city, developed. Originally, the site was used for habitation, but it had become a place of religious significance by the sixth century BC, when Pisistratus caused the building there of a **limestone temple of Athena**. The city's patron goddess was honoured in the Panathenaic Festival, which included athletic contests and a magnificent procession in which all the people of the city took part. The purpose of the Panathenaic procession was to deliver a new robe

pp. 24-25

The Parthenon from the north-west. From its position on the peak of the Acropolis, it dominates the entire basin of Attica and inspires awe with its inner strength, harmony and balance.

to cover the statue of Athena on the Acropolis, a ceremony which was accompanied by sacrifices on the Rock. The **Panathenaic Festival** was celebrated with the greatest pomp in the fifth century BC, when superb buildings were constructed on the Acropolis. In 437-432 BC, the architect Mnesicles constructed the monumental **Propylaea** at the west entrance to the Acropolis; the temple-like facade of this gateway would have instilled an attitude of piety in those who ascend-

ed towards the sacred buildings. At about the same time, Callicrates was responsible for the building of the Ionic amphiprostyle **temple of Athena Nike**, erected to commemorate the Athenian victory over the Persians. The **Parthenon**, symbol of democratic Athens, was completed between 447 and 432 BC, to plans by the architects Ictinus and Callicrates. Technically, the temple is a peripteral amphiprostyle structure (8 x 17), in the Doric order with Ionic features. The *cella* was unusually broad - thus marking a step forward in ancient Greek temple-building - and inside it was a two-storey colonnade in a Greek Π shape. In this was the famous and colossal chryselephantine statue of Athena Parthenos by the sculptor Phidias. The entire temple was built in marble from Mt Pendeli and was ornamented with the pioneering sculptural compositions of Phidias (on the east frieze: the battle of the Giants; on the west frieze: the

Phidias. Thanks to what archaeologists called its 'architectural refinements', by which they mean the curvature of its surfaces, the Parthenon gives the impression of being a piece of sculpture rather than a mere work of architecture. In this masterpiece of a building, all the ideological and artistic inquiries of the ancient Greeks came together and reached their solution in a single work. In 421-406 BC, the **Erechtheum** was built to the north of the Parthenon. This unusual Ionic temple was dedicated to the old gods of Athens and also to Poseidon and Athena, the deities who - according to the traditions - had quarrelled over which of them was to be the patron of the city. In the south porch of the Erechtheum stood the Caryatids, sculptures of the *kore* type whose purpose was to support the roof of the temple. Among the numerous other

p. 26

Above: the Ionic temple of Athena Nike and part of the Propylaea, on the Acropolis of Athens.

battle of the Amazons; on the south frieze: the battle of the Centaurs; on the north frieze: the fall of Troy; on the east pediment: the birth of Athena; on the west pediment: the dispute between Poseidon and Athena). The famous Ionic interior frieze, which showed the Panathenaic procession, was also the work of

buildings on the Acropolis were the **Sanctuary of Aphrodite Pandemos, the Sanctuary of Artemis of Brauron, the Chalcotheke, the temple of Rome and Augustus, the Sanctuary of Zeus Polieus** and the **Arrephorium.** In among these buildings were statues of the greatest value dedicated by followers of the various cults.

ACROPOLIS MUSEUM

In the south-east corner of the Acropolis is the **Acropolis Museum,** which is an ideal place for the visitor to gain an idea of the way in which Classical sculpture developed. Of particular interest are the statuary from the pediments of some of the small Archaic treasuries (or houses) which stood on the Acropolis (Heracles with the Hydra of Lerna, lions devouring a bull, the Apotheosis of Heracles on Olympus, the Olive Pediment, a three-bodied demon and Heracles wrestling with Triton) and the sculptures from the pediment of the Archaic temple of Athena, showing the Battle of the Giants (6th century BC). The Acropolis Museum has an extensive collection of *kores,* those works so characteristic of Archaic art (the Peplos *kore,* the Lyon *kore,* the Chios *kore,* the *kore* of Antenor). Among the works of sixth century art, special places are occupied by the Moschophoros, the Rampin horseman and a statue of Athena, seated, which was executed by the famous sculptor Endoeus. The period of the severe order (early fifth century BC) is represented by the Blonde Youth, the Boy of Critias, the Mourning Athena, and the *kore* by the sculptor Euthydicus. The most important exhibits in the Museum are, of course, the sculptures from the Parthenon, and in particular the relief slabs from the Ionic frieze. These are works of unique value, which constitute the Classical ideal at its absolute peak. In the last room are four of the six Caryatids from the Erechtheum.

The important monuments of the Acropolis are not confined to the top of the rock: some of the major finds have been made on its **south slopes**. Here stood the **sanctuary of Dionysus of Eleutherae**, with the **Theatre of Dionysus** where the great ancient dramatists first presented their works (fifth/fourth century BC: the construction of the first stone theatre; thereafter successive stages of conversion and repair until Roman times). To the east of the theatre, a few traces have survived of the **Odeum of Pericles**, a building of unusual circular design where musical contests were held (447-442 BC). To the west, archaeologists have uncovered the **Asclepium** of Athens, which was inaugurated in 420 BC. Nearby were **two choregic monuments** (those of Thrasyllus and Nicias - 319 BC), erected by the sponsors who had been victorious in drama contests. Many more of these choregic monuments stood along what is called the Street of the

p. 26

Below: the Ionic temple of Erechtheus, with the south porch of the Caryatids, on the Acropolis of Athens.

p. 27

Part of the north Ionic frieze of the Parthenon: the relief with the horsemen (Acropolis Museum).

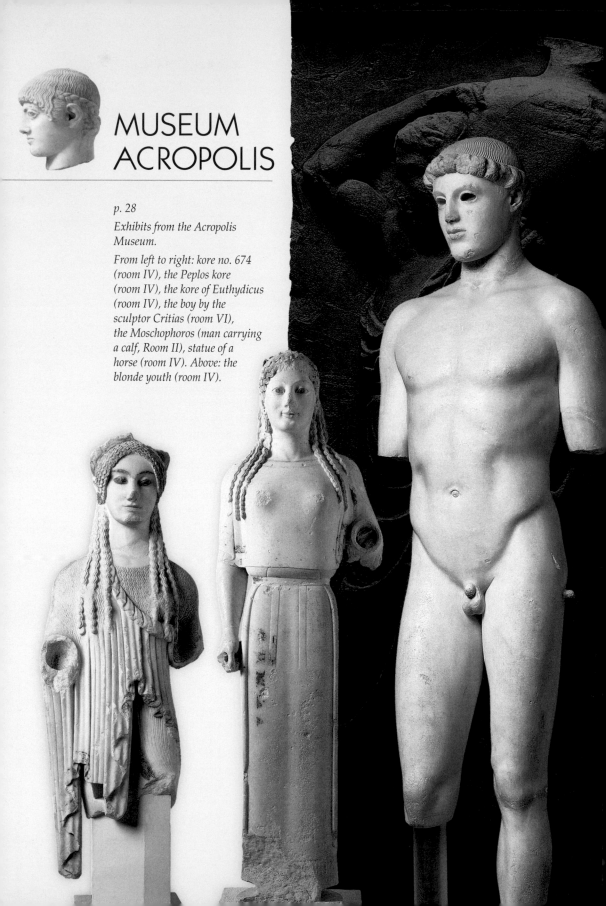

MUSEUM
ACROPOLIS

p. 28

Exhibits from the Acropolis Museum.

From left to right: kore no. 674 (room IV), the Peplos kore (room IV), the kore of Euthydicus (room IV), the boy by the sculptor Critias (room VI), the Moschophoros (man carrying a calf, Room II), statue of a horse (room IV). Above: the blonde youth (room IV).

p. 30

View of the Theatre of Dionysus as it is today. The coloured marble paving of the orchestra dates from Roman times.

p. 31

View of the Acropolis from the south-west. In the second century AD, the Odeum of Herodes Atticus was built on the south side of the Acropolis.

Tripods, sections of which - with the superb choregic monument of Lysicrates (334 BC) - have been discovered in Plaka. On the south side of the Acropolis there was also a long **stoa**, erected at the expense of King **Eumenes II** of Pergamum (2nd century BC). The imposing structure called the **Odeum of Herodes Atticus** (160-174 AD), dedicated to the memory of its founder's wife, Regilla, stands nearby; in the summer months, it is still a venue for artistic events.

The remains of the **ancient Agora** of Athens, which was the political and administrative centre of the city and the focus of all its social, commercial and religious activities, have been excavated on the north side of the Acropolis. The most northerly structure in the Agora is the **Poikile (painted) Stoa**, whose foundations are actually outside the fenced archae-

ological site. It was built around 460 BC and ornamented with works by some of the most famous painters of the time, including Polygnotus and Panaenus. The monuments on the west side of the archaeological site include: the **Royal stoa** (6th century BC), headquarters of the Archon-King, the **Stoa of Zeus** (5th century BC), the **Ionic temple of Apollo Patroös** (4th century BC), the **Metroön**, or temple where Rhea-Cybele, mother of the gods, was worshipped and where the city archives were kept (2nd century BC), the **Bouleuterium** (late 5th century BC), and the **Tholos**, a circular building for administrative and, probably, religious uses (5th century BC). Nearby, on the hill of Colonnus in the Agora, was built in the mid-fifth century BC the monumental **Temple of Hephaestus and Athena Erganes** (patrons of artisans), usually - though mistakenly - called the Theseum. This is a Doric peripteral temple with superb sculptural ornamentation (on the pediments: the Battle of the Centaurs to the east, the Fall of Crete on the west; the feats of Theseus and Heracles on the friezes). Inside were kept statues of the deities worshipped in the temple, by the sculptor Alcamenes. In the triangular main square of the Agora, bounded by the **Panathenaic Way** on the west side, stood an **altar to the cult of the twelve gods** (522/1 BC), the Doric **temple of Ares** (5th century BC), the **Precinct of the Eponymous Heroes** with the statues of the heroes who gave their names to the ten tribes of Attica (mid-4th century BC), the **Altar of Zeus of the Agora**, and the **Odeum**, which was constructed in 15 BC by Agrippa, son-in-law of Augustus (the building was modified in the second and fifth centuries AD, and became

the 'Gymnasium of the Giants'). The south side of the Agora was occupied by two stoas of the second century AD (the **Middle Stoa** and **South Stoa II**), the premises of the **Helaea**, the most important court of Athens after the fifth century BC, the **Ennea-krounos**, or nine-spouted fountain (dating from the time of Pisistratus), and a **Nymphaeum** which was a gift from Hadrian. To the east was the **Stoa of Attalus**, donated by Attalus II, King of Pergamum (150 BC). The Stoa has been reconstructed and houses an archaeological collection, among the most notable exhibits in which are a cult statue of Apollo Patroös by the sculptor Euphranor (4th century BC), important prehistoric finds, funerary

offerings from Geometric burials, inscriptions, items connected with the military organisation and public life of Athens, and vases in both the black and red-figure orders.

On the north-western outskirts of the city of Athens was the Kerameikos, the cemetery which contained the tombs of private citizens and those who had fallen in battle. This must have been an awe-inspiring place throughout the period when it was in use, for the tombs were adorned with outstanding art-works: statues and *stelae*. Casts of these now stand on the site itself, while the originals are kept in the **Kerameikos Museum**, together with the funerary offerings from inside the tombs. Through the Kerameikos ran the **walls** of Athens,

p. 32
View of the ancient Agora of Athens. To the left is the Stoa of Attalus, now the Museum of the Agora.

which divided the site into the Inner and Outer Kerameikos. The two main gates, the **Dipylon** and the **Sacred Gate**, were also here. The road which passed through the Sacred Gate was the **Sacred Way**, which ran west to Eleusis, while that which used the Dipylon was simply called the **Dromos** - 'the road'. The building known as the **Pompeium**, between the two gates, was the starting-place for the Panathenaic Procession, which followed the Dromos into the Agora before winding up to the Acropolis. Some remains of the Pompeium and of the gates have survived in the Kerameikos site, together with sections of the city wall in which the successive phases of repairs can be seen (479/8 BC, 394/3 BC, 253-60 AD, 6th century AD).

To the north-west of the Acropolis rises the rocky hill of the **Areopagus**, which after the seventh century BC was the seat of the admnistrative and judicial body of the same name. It was on the Areopagus that St Paul preached to the Athenians in 49/50 AD. To the west of the Sacred Rock was the **Pnyx**, where the *ecclesia* of the *deme* (that is, the assembly of the people) met after the sixth century BC. Further to the south was the **Hill of the Muses**, known today as Philopappos Hill from the funerary monument to the Roman Gaius Julius Antiochus Philopappus which was erected on its summit in 115 AD. Another nearby hill was dedicated to the **Nymphs**, and it was there that the Observatory of Athens was built in the nineteenth century.

p. 33
The temple of Hephaestus, one of the best-preserved monuments in Athens, in the ancient Agora. It dates from the mid-fifth century BC.

The area by the bed of the Ilissus river is notable for one of the most striking monuments in Athens, the **temple of Olympian Zeus**. Work on this temple, in the Doric order, began in the time of the Pisistratids (6th century BC), but the structure was only completed - in the Corinthian order - under Hadrian (131/2 AD). In order to welcome their benefactor the Roman Emperor to the inauguration of the temple he had finally finished, the Athenians erected the triumphal **Arch of Hadrian**; it still stands there today, beside one of the busiest streets in Athens.

In the Roman period (1st century BC), a new **agora** was built to the east of the ancient commercial area; this is also known as the **Forum of Caesar and Augustus**, or just as the **Roman Forum**. The Roman Forum occupied a rectangular area surrounded by Ionic porticoes. Further to the east, the astronomer Andronicus Cyrrhestes erected a structure which was simultaneously a water-clock, a solar clock, a weathervane and a planetarium and which bore reliefs of the eight winds personified on its exterior (the 'Tower of the Winds', 1st century AD). To the north of the Roman Forum was the **Library of Hadrian**, a monumental building surrounded by porticoes. Here there were luxurious reading-rooms and lecture halls, and in the courtyard was a pond around which the scholars could take their ease.

p. 34

Above: the water-clock of Andronicus Cyrrhestes or Tower of the Winds, in the Roman Agora.

Below: view of the Street of Tombs in the Kerameikos Cemetery: a marble bull from the funerary monument of Dionysios.

p. 35

View of the temple of Olympian Zeus; in the background, the Acropolis of Athens.

BYZANTINE PERIOD

In the early Byzantine period, many of the Classical monuments of Athens were converted into Christian churches. New churches were built, too, mostly in the basilica type. However, it was in the Middle Byzantine period (843-1204) that building activity was at its height. The most notable features of the Byzantine churches of Athens are the so-called 'Athenian cupola' with its elongated but elegant drum, the plainness of the external surfaces, and the use of brick courses in the masonry. Almost all these buildings are of the cross-in-square type. The finest examples of the Athenian churches are those of **St Nicholas 'Rangavas'** in Plaka (1031-1050), **Kapnikarea** (mid-11th century), **Sts Theodore** (1065), the main church of **Kaisariani Monastery** (late 11th century), **Our Lady 'Gorgoepikoos'** (12th century, now a chapel to Athens Cathedral), and the church of the **Holy Apostles**, built around 1000 in the ancient Agora in an unusual architectural type with four apses. In the octagonal type of ecclestiastical architecture are the **Russian church** ('Sotira Lykodimou'), dating from 1030, and the main church of Dafni Monastery (11th century). **Dafni Monastery** stands on the Sacred Way, on a site formerly occupied by a temple of Apollo Daphneius. This monument is of the greatest significance because of its mosaics, in which links to the aesthetic values of antiquity can be distinguished. For a collection of portable treasures of Byzantine Athens, we must go to the **Byzantine Museum**.

p. 36 - 37
View of the Academy of Athens, in the city centre.

On the **ground floor** are sculptures in stone and wood, icons, and wall-paintings. In **three of the rooms** are reconstructions of an Early Christian basilica, a cross-in-square church of the main Byzantine period, and a single-aisled post-Byzantine church.

Upstairs are more sculptures and icons, wall-paintings detached from defunct churches, miniature works of art, utensils and ecclesiastical robes.

FRANKISH AND TURKISH RULE - THE MODERN PERIOD

When Constantinople fell to the Crusaders ('Franks') in 1204, Athens was seized by Otto de la Roche of Burgundy, passing during the fourteenth century through the successive hands of the Catalans, the Florentine family of the Acciajuoli, the Venetians and the Byzantines. In 1458, the city was taken by the Turks, and the Acropolis became a Turkish settlement. In 1687, during the Turkish-Venetian wars, the Acropolis was bombarded and captured by the Venetian admiral Francesco Morosini. In 1690, Athens was back in Turkish hands, where it stayed until final liberation in 1833 and its recognition as capital of the modern Greek state. Important relics of the Greek struggle for freedom and of the history of modern Greece are to be seen in the **Historical and Ethnological Museum of Athens**, housed in the Old Parliament building (1858-1871). The modern history of Athens can also be traced in the **Vouros-Eftaxias Museum**.

After the proclamation of Athens

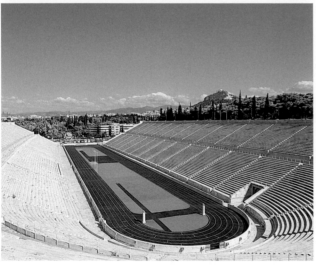

p. 38

Above: The monument to the Unknown Soldier, in front of the Greek Parliament.

Above:

Below: The Panathenaic Stadium.

as capital of Greece, the city was re-designed to plans by the architects Kleanthis and Schaubert. Most of the buildings constructed at this time were in the neo-Classical style, and many of them have survived to give a hint of a different atmosphere to the modern city. Among the most notable nineteenth-century buildings are **Parliament**, originally the palace of Othon, first King of Greece, the

Zappeio Conference Centre (1874-1888) in the **National Gardens**, the **Academy** (1859-1887), **Athens University** (1839-1864) and the **National Library** (1877-1902). There are numerous old mansion houses in the Plaka district of town, a charming area where we can gain a taste of what Athens must once have been like. Also in Plaka is the **Museum of Greek Folk Art**, which provides an

overview of the Greek vernacular tradition and folklore. Among other interesting sights in the city are **Mt Lycabettus,** with its little chapel to St George and the modern open-air theatre, **Omonia Square** in the heart of Athens, the **National Technical University** (1862-1876), **Syntagma Square** with its shops, the **Panathenaic Stadium**, a reconstruction of the ancient Stadium built to house the first Olympics of modern times in 1896, the **National Gallery**, with fine collections of the art of Greece and other countries, and the **Music Megaron**, a new concert-hall with outstanding acoustics. Athens today, with a population of more than 4 million, is very much the centre of Greece, not only geographically but also as the focus of almost all the country's important activities.

p. 39
The Zappeio Conference Centre.

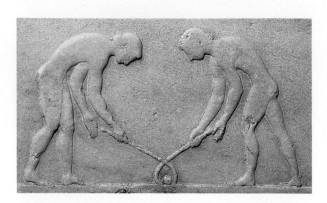

p. 40

Above: a scene of a sporting contest, from the base of a kouros (late sixth century BC).

Below: marble statuette of a flautist from the Cyclades (early Bronze Age).

p. 41

Left: the Archaic kouros no. 3851, known as the Anavyssos kouros.

Right: gold Mycenaean items.

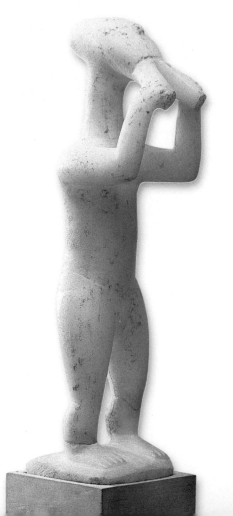

NATIONAL ARCHAEOLOGICAL MUSEUM

The history of the art not only of ancient Athens but of all of Greece can be seen in the halls of the **National Archaeological Museum**, housed in a neo-Classical building constructed in the nineteenth century. The prehistoric collection is in rooms 4, 5 and 6 on the ground floor. **Room 5** has Neolithic finds, **Room 6** artefacts of the Cycladic civilisation, and **Room 4** the stunning finds from Mycenae itself and other Mycenean sites. In **Rooms 7-13** we see the way in which sculpture evolved during the Archaic period. Of special interest are the *kouroi*, superb examples of Archaic art (the *kouroi* of Sunium, Anavyssos and of Ptoön, the young Aristodicus). An important collection of funerary and commemorative *stelae* from the Classical period is on display in **Rooms 14, 16, 17 and 18**, while **Room 15** is dominated by the wonderful bronze statue of Poseidon (or Zeus) found in the sea off Cape Artemisium and attributed to the sculptor Calamis (severe style). Among the most striking exhibits in **Room 21** is the Diadoumenos, a Late Hellenistic copy of an important lost work by Polyclitus. **Room 22** is given over to sculptures from the temple of Asclepius and the Tholos at Epidaurus (4th century BC). **Rooms 23-28** contain characteristic examples of the funerary *stelae* of the fourth century BC. In the centre of Room 27 is

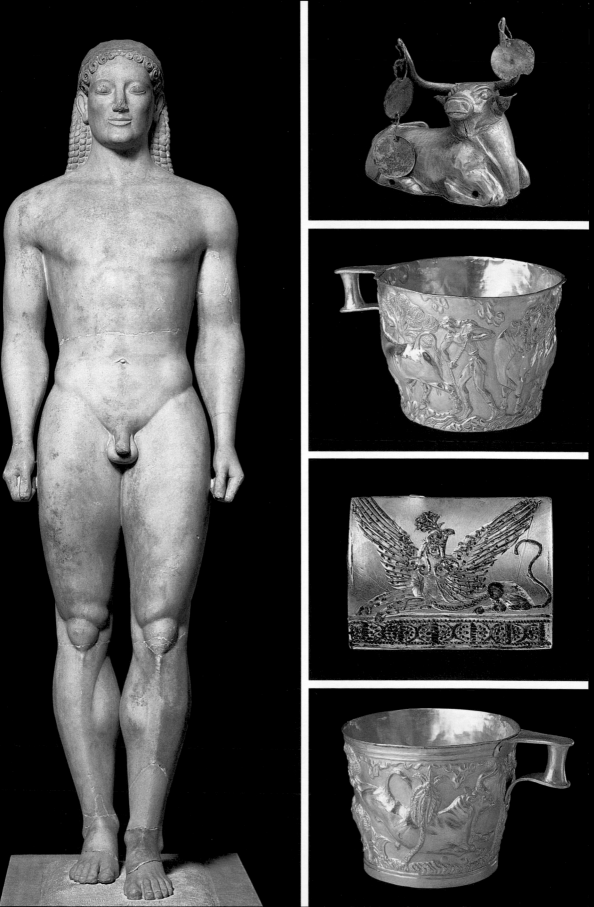

p. 42

Left: Geometric amphora from a funerary monument near the Dipylon Gate (eighth century BC).

Centre: red-figure Attic pelike.

Right: the Nessus amphora, a black-figure vase of the late seventh century.

p. 43

Bronze statue of Zeus or Poseidon found off Cape Artemisium, a work in the 'austere' style (room 15).

a bronze statue of a youth found in the sea off Anticythera and influenced by the art of Polyclitus (340 BC). Hellenistic sculpture occupies **Rooms 29-30**, and an interesting Roman collection has recently been installed in **Rooms 31-33**. The bronze exhibits in the Museum are concentrated in **Rooms 36-37**, and are notable for their wide typological variety and the skill of their miniature depictions. Note, in particular, the outstanding bronze statue of a youth, or possibly of Hermes (4th century BC), found at Marathon. In **Rooms 49-56,** on the upper floor, is a vast collection of pottery covering the era from the Geometric period to the 4th century BC, including some of the finest examples of black-figure and red-figure vases to be seen anywhere in the world. **Room 48** contains a prehistoric collection of the greatest importance, consisting of the pottery and wall-paintings from the settlement at Acrotiri on Thera (1550-1500 BC).

More examples of the art of the prehistoric era are to be seen in the **Goulandris Museum of Cycladic Art**, which as the name suggests, concentrates primarily on the artefacts of the Cycladic civilisation. The **Numismatic Museum** of Athens is housed in the Troy House ('Iliou Melathron'), built by Ernst Ziller as the residence of Heinrich Schliemann. Important collections of works from the prehistoric period to the time of Byzantium are also to be seen in the **Kanellopoulos Museum** and the **Benaki Museum.**

PIRAEUS

Piraeus is the third-largest city in Greece and its most important harbour. The area was first settled - according to the Hippodamian system of town planning - in the time of Themistocles, when the **Long Walls** (478 BC) were built, and it became especially important when Athens emerged as a naval power. Ancient Piraeus had two harbours, **Zea** and **Munichia**, the latter now known as Mikrolimano or Tourkolimano. Above Mikrolimano stands **Castella hill**, with pretty neighbourhoods and a chapel of the Prophet Elijah on its top. Two ancient theatres have come to light in Piraeus, along with traces of the ancient fortifications. The most important finds from the area can be seen in the city's **Archaeological Museum**; among them are three bronze statues, of Apollo (530 BC), Athena (4th century BC), and Artemis (4th century BC). Also of interest is the **Nautical Museum**, showing the maritime history of Greece from antiquity down to the present day.

ELEUSIS

Eleusis (modern Elefsina) stands in a flat part of Attica known as the Thriasian Plain. Human habitation in the area dates back to the Bronze Age, and the influence of Athens began in Mycenean times. In antiquity, Eleusis was the setting for mystical rites in honour of the deity Demeter, goddess of agriculture. The ceremonies had their beginnings in the myth according to which Demeter's daughter Persephone was abducted by Pluto, king of the underworld. After nine days of searching for her daughter, Demeter arrived in Eleusis, where she was treated kindly by Celeus, the king. With the mediation of Zeus, agreement was reached that Persephone would be allowed to return to her mother - but only for six months of the year, staying in Hades for the rest of her time. The Eleusians set up a sanctuary in honour of Demeter and her daughter, and the mysteries were performed their without interruption into Roman times. The Eleusinian Mysteries, which attracted initiates from all over the Greek world, lasted nine days. They began with a procession which made its way down the **Sacred Way** to Athens, returning to the sanctuary of the goddess after purification and sacrifices. The Mysteries were held in the building called the *Telesterium*,

p. 45

Above: the Ninnion tablet, showing scenes from the Eleusinian Mysteries (Elefsina Museum).

pp. 46-47
The temple of Poseidon at Sunium. The rocky hill on which it stands affords a fine view of the sunset.

◄ *p. 44*
The commercial harbour, Piraeus.

Below: bronze statue of Athena (fourth century BC, Piraeus Archaeological Museum).

◄ *p. 45*
Below: view of the archaeological site of ancient Eleusis; the Telesterium from the south.

and they seem to have created in the initiates a sense of heightened tension with spiritual and intellectual elevation. Even today, we do not know exactly what took place during the Mysteries. On the site in Elefsina, which is now a modern industrial city, there are remains of the Telesterium and of many other buildings connected with the rites. The **Archaeological Museum** of the town has important finds from the site.

SUNIUM (SOUNIO)

Cape Sunium is the most southerly extremity of Attica. On the cliff that towers out of the sea there, the Athenians worshipped Poseidon and Athena even as far back as the Geometric period. The first **temple of Poseidon** was built in the late sixth century BC, and was destroyed by the Persians in 480. In its place, Pericles ordered the construction (444-440 BC) of a marble peripteral temple in the Doric order, ornamented with friezes showing scenes from the Battle of the Centaurs, the Battle of the Giants and the feats of Theseus. The **temple of Athena** was built in the Archaic period, in the form of a simple *cella* with four Ionic columns in its interior. In 460-450 BC, Ionic colonnades were added to the east and west facades. In 412 BC, the sanctuaries at Sunium were fortified and the **wall** extended right round the temple of Poseidon. This became one of the most important fortresses in Attica, and had a permanent garrison. Bastions and ship-sheds were added in the third century BC.

Today, Sunium is one of the most popular archaeological sites in Greece. Apart from its historical interest, there is a superb view over the Aegean, and the sunset can often be unforgettable.

LAURIUM (LAVRIO) and THORIKOS

In antiquity, **Laurium** (modern Lavrio) was of decisive importance for the history of Athens because beneath it lay rich deposits of lead and silver. The income from the mines of Laurium allowed the Athenians to strengthen their naval power and create the miracle of the fifth century BC. At Kamariza, near the modern town, interesting ruins of the ancient mining installations have survived.

Close to Lavrio is **Thorikos**, a site occupied even in prehistoric times and later a centre for the processing of the ore mined at Laurium. Among the ruins of the ancient settlement are what has remained of one of the earliest surviving Greek **theatres**. It took the shape we see today in the sixth and fifth century BC, with an elliptical *orchestra* and *cavea*. The **temple and altar of Dionysus**, to the west of the theatre, also date from the fifth century BC.

p. 48
Fourth-century BC relief showing the goddess Artemis receiving the offerings of worshippers (Brauron Archaeological Museum).

BRAURON (VRAVRONA)

Brauron is located on the east coast of Attica, in a fertile valley which in ancient times was watered by the river Erasinus. The first human habitation dates back to about 3500 BC, and in the ninth century BC the **sanctuary of Artemis** was built on the banks of the Erasinus. Here the custom of *arcteia* was honoured, in accordance with which young girls, who were known as 'bears' (*arctoi*) stayed for a while with the goddess preparing for married life and child-bearing. Also worshipped at Brauron was Iphigenia, who was traditionally believed to have stayed a while in the sanctuary before dying. In the archaeological site, we can see the ruins of the so-called **cenotaph of Iphigenia**, of a Doric **temple of Artemis** (5th century BC) and of a **Doric stoa** where the 'bears' lived, the earliest Π-shaped colonnade yet found in Greece (420 BC). The offerings of the faithful and other finds from the site can be seen in the interesting **Museum of Brauron**.

MARATHON

Marathon is a small town standing in a fertile plain which leads down to the Bay of Marathon. Man first lived here in prehistoric times; a **cave at Oinoi** near Marathon, where there was a cult of the god Pan in the fifth century, has yielded traces of Neolithic habitation. A settlement dating from the early part of the Bronze Age has come to light at the

spot called **Plasi**, while **Tsepi** has yielded one of the best-preserved cemeteries of the early Bronze Age. At **Vrana**, four Middle Helladic and Mycenean mounds have been excavated, and a nearby **tholos tomb** produced royal grave offerings.

Marathon is best known, however, for the battle in the vicinity in 490 BC, when the Greeks triumphed over the Persians. The Greek army was made up chiefly of Athenians and men of Plataeae, and the large force they faced consisted of *hoplites* or infantrymen, archers and mounted knights. Miltiades of Athens, commanding the Greeks, skilfully managed to surprise the Persian army and force it on to the

retreat, turning the invaders back to their ships in Marathon Bay. The Athenians chose the spot where the last clashes between the two sides had taken place as the burial-ground for their dead, over whose tombs they erected a **mound** which can still be seen today. Another such mound, discovered at Vrana, is believed to have contained the fallen of Plataeae. At Marathon there is an **Archaeological Museum** with finds from prehistoric times to the Roman period.

To the west of the town of Marathon is Marathon lake, from which the water supply of Athens is piped. The lake has a fine marble-faced dam built early in the twentieth century.

p. 49

The Doric Stoa in the archaeological site at Brauron, 420 BC. It consists of three wings in a Π-shape. At the far ends of the west and north wings were rooms in which visitors were accommodated.

RAMNOUS
(RAMNOUNDAS)

The ancient *deme* of Ramnous was on the shores of the Euboean Gulf, to the north-east of Athens. Archaeological excavations have brought to light many of the **houses** of the community, the main street lined with **funerary monuments**, a **fortress or guard-post**, an early **theatre** inside the fortress, and a **sanctuary of the god Amphiaraus.**

Ramnous was known in antiquity as the location of the **cult of the goddess Nemesis**, who protected balance and moderation in the world and punished those who dared to disturb them. In the archaeological site of Ramnous we can see the ruins of the temple of Nemesis, in all the various stages of building through which it went. The last stage, dating from 430-420 BC, contained the famous statue of Nemesis by the sculptor Agoracritus.

OROPOS -
THE AMPHIARAEIO

Near Oropos, to the north of Athens, was the sanctuary of the healer-god Amphiaraus, which was founded in the late fifth century BC. According to the myths, Amphiaraus was king of Argos and took part in the campaign mounted by Polynices to dislodge his brother Eteocles from the throne of Thebes. When the campaign failed, Amphiaraus fled to Attica with his enemies in hot pursuit - and as they were about to kill him, Zeus unleashed a thunderbolt which split open the earth, into which

Amphiaraus vanished, to emerge later from a spring. At that point, the people of Oropos built a sanctuary, which developed into the political and therapeutic centre of their city. Those in search of a cure for their illnesses or a solution to their problems slept on a goat-skin and the advice of Amphiaraus was vouchsafed to them in their dreams. The remains of the **Amphiaraeion** can be seen today in an attractive ravine near Oropos.

p. 50
The temple of Nemesis at Ramnous, fifth century BC.

p. 51
Funerary stele from the sanctuary of Nemesis at Ramnous.

THE ISLANDS
OF THE SARONIC GULF

Salamis (Salamina)

Salamis is the island closest to the coast of Attica. To the north is the bay of Eleusis, with much industrial development which has had an impact on the physiognomy of the island. Salamis was first inhabited in the Neolithic period, and in the myths was the home of Telamon and his son Ajax, the latter of whom played an important part in the Trojan War. It was also the birthplace of the tragic poet Euripides.

Salamis is known in history for the sea-battle fought off its coast in 480 BC. The Persian king, Xerxes, first occupied the empty city of Athens - whose inhabitants had taken refuge in the surrounding countryside - and was manipulated into giving battle against the Greek fleet in the strait between Salamis and the mainland. The choice of this watery battlefield was the result of the perseverence of Themistocles of Athens, who reasoned - rightly - that the narrow strait would make it difficult for the large and numerous Persian ships to manoeuvre. During the battle, most of the Persian vessels were sunk or damaged, and their navy suffered a blow from which it never recovered.

Aegina

Aegina took its name from a nymph who was the mother of Aeacus, one of the Judges of the Underworld. According to the myths, Aeacus was the sole human survivor of a flood, but he found his solitude hard to bear and so sought the help of Zeus. Zeus turned the ants of the island into human beings, the Myrmidons, to keep Aeacus company. His sons were Peleus, father of Achilles, and Telamon, father of Ajax, who soon moved away from the island - to Thessaly and Salamis, respectively.

Aegina was first inhabited in the third millenium BC. An important **prehistoric settlement** has been discovered at **Kolona**. There were ten successive building phases in the history of this settlement, ending in the late prehistoric period, and it was first fortified in about 2200 BC. Nearby, in the sixth century BC, a Doric **temple of Apollo** was built, of which a single column has survived.

The most important temple on the

p. 52
Aegina, one of the most popular islands in the Saronic Gulf.

p. 53
Above: the temple of Aphaea, Aegina. In the background, Ayia Marina.

Below: view of Aegina harbour.

island, and one of the best-preserved in mainland Greece, was dedicated to **Aphaea**, a deity with pre-Greek roots. This is the most advanced of the Late Archaic temples yet discovered (constructed in 575-550 BC), and it foreshadows the later development of the Classical Doric order. It was peripteral, with two double colonnades in the *cella*, short proportions and architectural refinements to correct the visual impression. The pedimental sculptures showed scenes from the fighting between Greeks and Trojans flanking a central figure of Athena (now in the Glyptothek, Munich). The east pediment was replaced in the early fifth century BC by another composition on the same theme.

In antiquity, Aegina was famous for the work of its coppersmiths, the best-known of whom was called Onatas. Some of the ancient art-works of the island can be seen in the **Archaeological Museum** in Aegina town.

Poros

Poros actually consists of two islets (Sphairia and Kalavria) joined by a narrow neck of land and separated from the main bulk of the Peloponnese by a very narrow channel. The nature of the terrain thus gives the island a charm all its own. In antiquity, the people of Poros formed an Amphictyony, or religious league, the members of which were Aegina, Hermione, Epidaurus, Nauplio, Athens and Orchomenos. On Kalavria there was a **sanctuary of Poseidon**, consisting of a sixth-century **temple** of the god and the **Amphictyony buildings**. Tradition tells us that the Athenian orator Demosthenes took

pp. 54-55

Views of the pretty island of Poros. Thanks to its beautiful landscapes, dense greenery and mild climate, the island is very popular with visitors.

his own life in the temple of Poseidon when he was pursued to the island by his political opponents in 322 BC.

Hydra

Hydra is a uniquely attractive place, thanks to its barren, rocky terrain and the unusual nature of its town and buildings. The island attracts many visitors, and has a particularly cosmopolitan atmosphere. It was inhabited in ancient times, but never flourished then as it was to in the seventeenth and eighteenth centuries, when the islanders were the owners of a large merchant fleet which plied throughout the Mediterranean. The ships and their experienced mariners (A. Miaoulis, the Kountouriotis brothers, I. Tombazis and others) made an

p. 56

Above: the port of Hydra. The plain stone houses of the little town, clinging to the bare rock, create an unforgettable impression.

Below: view of Spetses.

p. 57

View of Hydra.

inestimable contribution to the Greek War of Independence of 1821. Traces of the maritime tradition can still be seen today in the **old harbour**, the **mansions** of the old sea-faring families and the modern **Merchant Navy Training School**. The **Tombazis mansion** now operates as a branch of the School of Fine Arts in Athens, and has an interesting collection of art-works on the theme of the Greek War of Independence.

Spetses

Known in antiquity as Pityusa, Spetses was inhabited as far back as the Bronze Age, as we know from finds in the area of **Ayia Marina**. In the seventeenth century, its inhabitants, like those of Hydra, began to earn their living from the sea, and they, too, contributed much to the success of the War of Independence. Laskarina Bouboulina, one of the heroines of the Struggle, was a woman of Spetses. The history of the island can be traced in the exhibits of the **Hadziyannis-Mexis Museum,** which has an interesting archaeological, historical and folklore collection.

THEBES (THIVA)

According to tradition, Thebes was founded by Cadmus, who arrived in the area in search of his sister Europa. His city was initially named Cadmeia, taking the name by which it was later known from Thebe, daughter of Asopus. Among the descendants of Cadmus was Laius, whose family became the nucleus of one of the most important mythological cycles, familiar to us frm the works of the great ancient tragedians. Laius married Jocasta, and the fruit of their union was Oedipus. When the child was still a babe in arms, he was turned out of the palace for fear of an oracle which had pronounced that he was destined to kill his father and take his mother to bed.

When Oedipus grew up - far from his birthplace - he did indeed kill Laius, though without knowing his identity. At this time, Thebes was terrorised by a monster called the Sphinx, which asked each passer-by a riddle and killed him when he failed to find the answer to it.

Oedipus solved the riddle, and was awarded marriage to the widow Jocasta as a prize. When the tragic truth came out, Oedipus blinded himself with his own hands and went into exile (see *Oedipus Rex*). After he had gone, his sons Polynices and Eteocles fell out over who should occupy the throne, and

Polynices waged war on Thebes with the help of seven leaders of other Greek cities (see *Seven Against Thebes, Phoenician Women*). The brothers killed each other, but while Eteocles was buried with full honours, Creon, Jocasta's brother, forbade the burial of Polynices. Antigone, daughter of Polynices, objected to this ban and buried her brother in accordance with the laws of the gods - for which she was punished with death (see *Antigone*). At a later date, the sons of the original seven leaders marched once more against Thebes and destroyed the city.

Another cycle of the myths involves Dionysus, son of Zeus by Semele, daughter of Cadmus. Dionysus was born in Thebes but raised far from home, and when he returned to his birthplace he brought a new religion of his own with him. Pentheus, king of Thebes, opposed the cult of Dionysus and received divine punishment: his own mother, Agave, and the women of Thebes, in a frenzy of ecstasy caused by the wine of Dionysus, dismembered Pentheus and devoured him (see *Bacchae*).

The mythical tradition about Cadmus and the finds which archaeological investigations of modern Thiva have yielded tell us much about the city's importance in the Mycenean era. The Mycenean acropolis of Cadmeia occupied the site of an Early Helladic settlement and now lies beneath the centre of the modern city. Archaeologists hypothesise that the city was surrounded by a wall which we know to have been built in two phases. Sections of the **old Cadmeum** have been discovered beneath Pindarou St.

In the late fourteenth century BC, the old palace was destroyed and the **New Cadmeium** built in its place.

Traces of this (the **archive**, the **baths**, the **armoury**, **workshops,** etc.) have come to light in various parts of the town. The New Cadmeium was itself destroyed by fire in the mid-thirteenth century BC.

In the historical period, Thebes was an independent city-state in constant rivalry with nearby Orchomenos. Around 520 BC, Thebes and the surrounding cities set up the Boeotian Federation, which was in effect a defensive alliance to protect themselves against Athens and Thessaly. During the Persian Wars, Theban animosity towards Athens caused the city to help the invaders, while nearby Plataeae and Thespiae sided with the rest of the Greeks. It was at **Plataeae**, in 479 BC, that one of the most decisive Greek victories over the Persians took place, and after it the Thebans were displaced from their leadership of the Boeotian Federation and punished in other ways. The city now sided with Sparta against Athens, and after a short period of Athenian hegemony was soon back as the chief city in the Boeotian Federation (446 BC). During the Peloponnesian Wars, Thebes took the side of Sparta, but when the financial benefits which the Spartans had promised to it and other

p. 58

Above: two different types of Mycenean earthenware figurines found at the Kolonaki burial ground (Thebes Archaeological Museum, case 3).

Below: Archaic kouros from the sanctuary of Apollo at Ptoon in Boeotia (Thebes Archaeological Museum, no. 3).

p. 59

Red-figure scyphos by the 'Brygos painter' showing a Satyr (Thebes Archaeological Museum, case 7).

p. 60

Left: terracotta female figurines from the ancient burials at Tanagra (330-200 BC, Thebes Archaeological Museum, case 13).

Right: painted Mycenaean larnax from Tanagra; its upper band shows a hunting scene and the lower band the sport of bull-leaping (Thebes Archaeological Museum, room D, no. 1).

Greek cities failed to materialise, it changed sides. The Federation broke up in 386 BC, and in 382 Sparta installed an oligarchic government in Thebes. In 379, on the initiative of Pelopidas and Epaminondas, Thebes expelled the Spartan garrison, and in 377 joined the Second Athenian League. At the same time, Thebes became the leader in the founding of a new union of cities, the *Koinon* ('commune') of Boeotia, and came into conflict with Sparta again, a war which culminated in the battle of **Leuktra** in 371 BC. The victory won by Epaminondas in that battle proved decisive, and made Thebes the leading power in Greece for a while. Epaminondas advanced into the Peloponnese, allying Thebes with the Arcadians and Messenians, always traditional enemies of Sparta. In 370 and 369 BC, he founded Megalopolis and Messene, respectively, but after his death in 362 BC Thebes went into decline. In the fourth century BC, Thebes and Athens faced Philip of Macedon together. The heroism of the Sacred Band was unable to prevent Philip's victory at

Chaironeia in 338 BC, and the Macedonian king punished Thebes by installing an oligarchic regime in the city and putting a Macedonian garrison in the Cadmeum. At **Chaironeia** itself, a marble lion was placed on a high plinth as a memorial over the tomb of those who were killed in the battle; it can still be seen, restored. In 335 BC, Alexander occupied Thebes and burned the city, sparing only the house of the lyric poet Pindar. Rebuilding was completed in 316 BC by Cassander, king of Macedon, who refounded the *Koinon* of the Boeotians. In 197 BC, the city sided with Rome, and in 86 BC it was sacked by Sulla. In the Roman era, Thebes subsided into obscurity; we know that it was laid waste by the Goths in the third and fourth centuries AD. Under Byzantium, however, it flourished once again thanks to its production of silk, and under the 'Franks' it was fortified and served as the capital of a principality. The **Archaeological Museum** of modern Thiva is in Pindarou St and has an interesting collection of finds dating from prehistory to the Roman period. In the **entrance hall** there are Hellenistic and Roman reliefs and inscriptions; the exhibits of **Room A** include important sculptures and funerary *stelae*, including the fine *kouroi* found at the sanctuary of Apollo on Mt Ptoön. In **Room B,** the eye is drawn by the Mycenean finds from the Cadmeum and by the exhibits from the settlements, cemeteries and sanctuaries of historic Boeotia as well as from the sanctuary of the Cabiri, 8 km. to the west of Thebes, where mystical ceremonies took place. **Room C** contains sculpture dating from between the fifth century BC and the Roman period. **Room D** is devoted to the finds from the Mycenean **cemetery at Tanagra**; there are numerous terracotta sarcophagi painted with scenes connected with the rites for the dead.

OSIOS LOUKAS

The Monastery of the Blessed Luke ('Osios Loukas') - dedicated to a local saint, and not the Evangelist - is one of the most important monastic buildings anywhere in the Greek world. The Blessed Luke was a hermit in the area, known for his charitable works and miraculous powers. He died in 953, and was buried beneath his cell. Not long afterwards, his remains were moved to a cruciform house of prayer, and in 1011 the main church of the monastery, as we see it today, was finished and ready to serve as his tomb. Next to the the main church is the church of Our Lady, built sometime after 961 in honour of the Blessed Luke and to mark the fact that

p. 61

The katholikon of the Monastery of the Blessed Loukas (eleventh century) and the church of Our Lady (tenth century), from the east.

he had prophesied the recapture of Crete by the Byzantine Empire.

The **church of Our Lady** is the earliest surviving example of the composite cross-in-square type of church with a dome borne on four columns, and there is evidence that it was built with funds granted by the Byzantine Emperor. This is the oldest known church with a *lite* (that is, a two-columned narthex to the west) and with a dome of the so-called 'Athenian' type.

The *katholikon* (**main church**) of Osios Loukas is, in turn, the earliest known example of an octagonal church in the so-called Epirus type. The nave is covered by a broad dome which unifies the interior and gives it a spacious feel while letting in plenty of light. The bones of the saint are kept at the point where the main church

and that of Our Lady join. There are superb mosaics on the walls, notable for their anti-classical atmosphere and the emphasis on schematisation, distorted proportions and the spirituality of the figures depicted. The mosaics date from the 1030s. Similar characteristics can be distinguished in the wall-paintings in the chapels to the main church and in the underground cruciform **crypt of St Barbara**.

ORCHOMENOS-GLAS

The site of **Orchomenos** was first inhabited in the Neolithic period and the city grew to prominence in Mycenean times. Orchomenos was noted in antiquity for its wealth-Homer remarks upon it-which must have been the result of the cultivation of Copais, a marshy plain which the Minyans who lived in the city managed to drain so that it became fertile ground. Some sections of the **Mycenean acropolis** (14th-13th century BC) have come to light, together with many important artefacts. The most important monument of all, of course, is the so-called **Treasury of Minyas**, the tomb alleged to have been occupied by the mythical king of Orchomenos. This is one of the largest Mycenean *tholos* tombs ever found. Dating from the thirteenth century BC, it is one of the most advanced and carefully built structures of its time, and is very rare in having - like the 'Treasury of Atreus' at Mycenae - a lateral interior chamber. The

p. 62
The Resurrection, mosaic from the narthex of the church of the Blessed Loukas, eleventh century.

p. 63
The lion of Chaironeia, the monument erected to commemorate the victory of Philip II of Macedon in 338 BC.

inside of the tomb was decorated with bronze rosettes, while the ceiling of the side chamber had spirals in relief and plant motifs of outstanding artistry.

Close to the site of the Mycenean palace are the ruins of a **theatre** dating from the late fourth century, where musical contests in honour of the Graces and Dionysus were held. Also in the vicinity is the Byzantine church of **Our Lady 'Skripous'**, built in 873/4 in the transitional cruciform inscribed type. Building materials were taken from ancient Orchomenos for the construction of this church.

On the north-east side of the Copais plain, on a hill, stands **the fortress of Glas**, the largest Mycenean acropolis with a circuit of 'Cyclopean' walls. When the Minyans of Orchomenos drained Lake Copais, Glas on its hill was used as a lookout post to guard the fields and as a store where farm produce could be kept. The walls, some three kilometres in length, and the four gates have survived in relatively good condition. The fortress was built in the early thirteenth century and destroyed by fire less than a hundred years later.

According to traditions dating back to antiquity, **Lake Copais** was the largest lake in Greece, but it was always marshy. The Minyans of Orchomenos constructed drainage works of a kind never seen before and managed to farm the area, but by the historic period the lake was a marsh again. It was not until the end of the nineteenth century that reclamation was completed, with the construction of canals leading off the water from the rivers into the Gulf of Euboea.

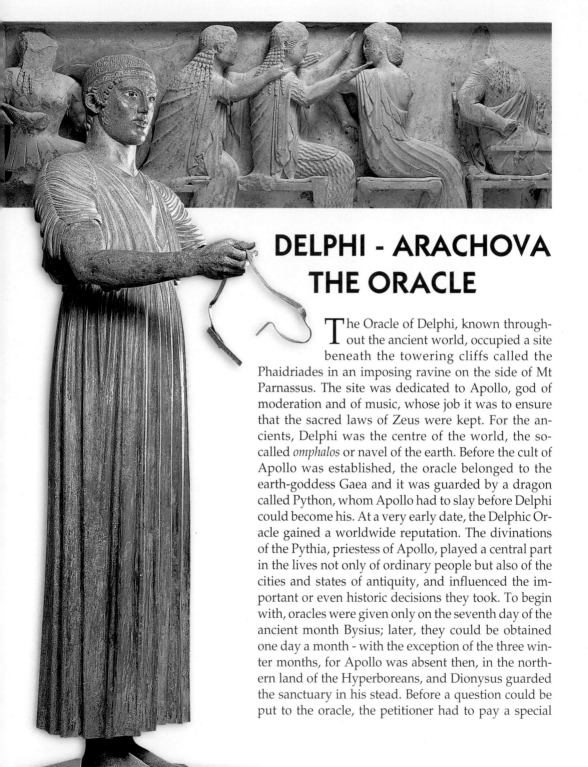

DELPHI - ARACHOVA
THE ORACLE

The Oracle of Delphi, known through-out the ancient world, occupied a site beneath the towering cliffs called the Phaidriades in an imposing ravine on the side of Mt Parnassus. The site was dedicated to Apollo, god of moderation and of music, whose job it was to ensure that the sacred laws of Zeus were kept. For the ancients, Delphi was the centre of the world, the so-called *omphalos* or navel of the earth. Before the cult of Apollo was established, the oracle belonged to the earth-goddess Gaea and it was guarded by a dragon called Python, whom Apollo had to slay before Delphi could become his. At a very early date, the Delphic Oracle gained a worldwide reputation. The divinations of the Pythia, priestess of Apollo, played a central part in the lives not only of ordinary people but also of the cities and states of antiquity, and influenced the important or even historic decisions they took. To begin with, oracles were given only on the seventh day of the ancient month Bysius; later, they could be obtained one day a month - with the exception of the three winter months, for Apollo was absent then, in the northern land of the Hyperboreans, and Dionysus guarded the sanctuary in his stead. Before a question could be put to the oracle, the petitioner had to pay a special

tax, purify himself and make sacrifices. The Pythia and her assistant priestesses washed at the Castallian spring, near the sanctuary, and then descended into the depths of the temple. The Pythia, seated on a copper tripod over a crevice in the ground, chewed laurel leaves and inhaled the vapours emerging from the earth. The god then spoke through her mouth, in a language which only the priests of the sanctuary could understand and interpret. His answers were often indefinite and ambiguous, but that in no way reduced popular respect for the wisdom of his judgement.

History

◄ p. 64
Above: part of the east frieze of the Treasury of the Siphnians at Delphi (525 BC, Delphi Archaeological Museum).
Below: the Charioteer of Delphi, one of the few surviving original bronze statues of the Classical period (474 BC, Delphi Archaeological Museum).

◄ p. 65
The Tholos at Delphi, 400-390 BC.

The area around Delphi was inhabited in Mycenean times, and by the eighth century BC had become a place of importance because of the reputation of the oracle. In the seventh century BC, the Delphic Amphictyony was formed: this was a religious federation whose purpose was to protect the interests of the sanctuary and the surrounding cities. In 600 BC, the Amphictyony declared the First Sacred War on the city of Crisa, which controlled access from the coast of the Corinthian Gulf and had been taxing pilgrims. In 582 BC, to celebrate their victory in this war, the people of Delphi revived the Pythian Games, contests for athletes and musicians which were held every four years and were of a Panhellenic nature. During the Persian Wars, the oracle was accused of discouraging the Greek side with its utterances, but afterwards the sanctuary received many rich offerings to commemorate the Greek victory. In 448-447 and 356-346 BC, in the Second and Third Sacred Wars, Delphi was victorious over Phocis, which had laid claim to ownership of the sanctuary. In the Third War - and also in the Fourth, against Amphissa in 339 BC - Philip II of Macedon intervened to settle the issue. After sacking Amphissa and defeating the Athenians and Thebans at Chaironeia in 338 BC, Philip was recognised as protector of the Delphic sanctuary, a title which passed to his son Alexander in 336. In 290 BC, ownership of Delphi came into the hands of the Aetolian League, which in 279 was able to successfully resist an incursion of Gauls. The Romans captured the area in 179 BC, and in 86 BC the shrine was looted by Sulla. In 67 BC, Nero carried many of the treasures of Delphi off to Rome, and Constantine the Great removed still more to Constantinople in the fourth century AD. The oracle itself was closed in 394 AD, by decree of the Byzantine Emperor Theodosius I. In modern times, the village of Kastri grew up on the site, and had to be moved further to the west in 1891, when the French Archaeological School began to excavate the ancient site.

The sanctuary of Apollo

The sanctuary of Apollo was surrounded by a **precinct**, built in the seventh century BC and reconstructed in the sixth. The main gate into the precinct lay on its west side, later being moved to the south-east, where the entry to the archaeological site is today. Here the **Sacred Way** began, winding up to the temple of Apollo and lined with the countless **votive statues** of Greek and foreign cities. Outside the precinct was the **Forum** of Roman times, and at the beginning of

the Sacred Way were some notable statues erected to commemorate famous victories won by the Arcadians of the Achaean League, the Spartans, the Athenians and the Argives.

Apart from these statues, it was also the custom for the city-states to constuet treasuries - small buildings in the shape of temples - in which the artefacts they dedicated were kept. In the late sixth century, the Doric **treasury of Sikyon** was built on a site previously occupied by a circular temple for the worship of Gaea (580 BC) and a single-winged Doric building of 560 BC. The Ionic, marble **treasury of the Siphnians** was a particularly splendid structure. It was built in 525 BC in gratitude to the god for the deposits of gold and silver which were mined on the island of Siphnos. On its facade, the treasury had two Caryatids rather than the usual columns, while its pediments and metopes bore superb sculptures and its door was ornamented with plant motifs in relief. Treasuries were also dedicated by **Megara, Thebes** (in 371 BC, after the battle of Leuctra), **Boeotia, Potidaea, Cnidus** (550-545 BC), Cypselus tyrant of **Corinth** (614-585 BC), and **Cyrene** (fourth century BC). One of the most striking buildings along the Sacred Way was the Doric **Treasury of the Athenians**, which has been restored. It was dedicated in 508-507 BC, after the overthrow of the Pisistratid tyranny and the restoration of democracy in

p. 67
The Treasury of the Athenians, one of the most imposing buildings along the Sacred Way through the archaeological site at Delphi. In Parian marble, it belongs to the Doric order. It has a sekos and a prodomos with two columns in antis (508-507 BC).

p. 68

Above: the theatre of Delphi in the form it took in the Roman period. The theatre could seat 5,000 and consisted of a cavea, an orchestra and a skene.

Below: the temple of Apollo. The members surviving today date from the fourth century BC.

Athens. On the frieze of the treasury were sculptures showing the feats of Heracles and Theseus, while commemorative inscriptions and two hymns to Apollo were built into the walls. In the **triangular space** in front of the treasury, the Athenians displayed their booty from the battle of Marathon. Further to the north were the **Bouleuterium** of Delphi (7th-6th century BC), the **Rock of the Sibyl**, on which the priestess of Gaea perched to deliver her oracles, the **Rock of Leto**, where Apollo and his mother Leto

slew the Python, and the **Sphinx of the Naxians**, which stood on a tall Ionic column after 650 BC. At this point was a circular open space, the **Halos** (threshing-floor), where the ceremony called the *Septeria* was performed in commemoration of the killing of Python. On the north-wide side of the Halos was the monumental **stoa of the Athenians**, built in 479 BC to house the loot won by the Athenians in their naval victories.

To the north of the stoa of the Athenians are the ruins of the most sacred

building at Delphi, the **temple of Apollo**. According to the tradition, the first three temples to stand on this site were built of laurel branches, beeswax, and feathers and metal. The first stone temple was erected in the seventh century BC by Trophonius and Agamedes. In the sixth century, it was replaced by a new building constructed after subscriptions had been raised in cities all over the known world. The largest sum of money was contributed by the exiled Athenian family of the Alcmaeonids, who took over the task of completing the temple in the period from 514/3 to 506/5 BC and gave it a marble facade on the east side; limestone had been used for the remainder of the building. This is an elongated Doric peripteral temple, with sculptures showing, on the west pediment, the Battle of the Giants and, on the east, the emergence of Apollo with his chariot. This temple was demolished in 373 BC by an earthquake, and work began immediately on the construction of a new one, which - with the help of all the Greeks - was

p. 69

The temple of Apollo of the fourth century BC was in the Doric order and consisted of a sekos, a pronaos to the east and an opisthodomos to the west.

completed in 330 BC. We are told that the architects were Spinthar, Xenodorus and Agathon. The new temple was also Doric and peripteral, with an *adyton*, an underground chamber at the back of the *cella* where the divination took place. In the *adyton* were a chasm in the ground, a laurel tree, the stone called 'the navel of the earth', a gold statue of Apollo and the tomb of Dionysus. The *cella*, which was unusually long, had two double colonnades; in it, the flame revered by all the Greeks burned perpetually on the altar of Hestia (Vesta). Outside the *cella*, in the *pronaos*, sayings of the Seven Sages of antiquity were carved on the walls. The pediments were designed by Praxias and Androsthenes; on the east side were Apollo, Leto and Artemis (the Delian Triad), and on the west was Dionysus with his entourage. Gold shields, captured at Marathon and during the victory over the Gauls, hung on the frieze. To the east of the temple was an **altar** dedicated by the people of Chios in gratitude at being granted the right to be the first to receive oracles. Further to the east were sumptuous **votive offerings** dedicated to Apollo by cities and private individuals. Nearby, on a flat piece of ground, was the Doric **stoa of Attalus I**, king of Pergamum (240-197 BC). On the northernmost edge of the temple precinct, archaeologists have uncovered the **house of Cnidus** (475-460 BC), where visitors to Delphi from that city in Asia Minor could meet. The house was ornamented with paintings by the great artist Polygnotus of Thasos.

To the north-west of the temple, the **theatre** of Delphi was built in the fourth century BC; it later had to be re-constructed, and Eumenes II modified it to give it a monumental appearance. What we see today are the foundations of the Roman theatre. Early in the twentieth century, the Greek poet Angelos Sikelianos and his American wife Eva revived the theatrical performances here as part of their campaign to make the sanctuary of Apollo a place of international brotherhood and reconciliation.

A path climbs up from the theatre to the **Stadium** of Delphi (late 4th - early 3rd century BC), where the Pythian Games were held. This is the best-preserved stadium anywhere in Greece, with traces of a monumental propylum to the east as well as the stone seats of the second century BC.

The sanctuary of Athena Pronaea

The second of the important sanctuaries at Delphi was dedicated to **Athena Pronaea**. The remains of its buildings have been excavated to the south-east of the sanctuary of Apollo, in an area which has yielded the earliest known traces of cult worship. A female divinity was worshipped here in Mycenean times, later being replaced by Athena. The sanctuary of Athena stood inside a walled precinct whose main entrance was on its north-east side. The first **temple** to the goddess was erected in the early sixth century and, unusually, faced south. It was Doric and peripteral, with an altar to the east. Late in the sixth century, a new Doric temple was constructed on the same site, accompanied by a monumental altar to the east of the earlier structure. In the same area **altars** have been discovered to Zeus Polieus, Athena Erganes, Athena

p. 71

The Sphinx of the Naxians, with a height of some 12 metres, was dedicated to Apollo by the people of Naxos in 560 BC. The mythical creature has the face of a woman, the body of a lion and the wings of a bird. It is one of the most important works of the Ionian school of sculpture (Delphi Archaeological Museum, room 2).

Zosteria, the goddess Eileithyia and Hygeia, the health goddess. To the west of the temple of Athena were two **treasuries**, one in the Doric order which imitated the treasury of the Athenians (475-470 BC) and one in the Ionic order dedicated by the people of Massalia (Marseilles) late in the sixth century. Still further to the west are the ruins of the **Tholos** of Delphi, a famous circular building designed by the architect Theodorus and built in 400-390 BC. There were 20 Doric columns round the exterior, and 10 Corinthian columns in the *cella*. The roof was conical, and the external frieze was ornamented with scenes from the Battle of the Centaurs and the Battle of the Amazons. The frieze of the *cella* bore sculptures depicting the feats of heroes and an assembly of the gods. To the west of the Tholos stood a **Doric temple** of 370-360 BC and a **rectangular building** of the fourth century BC whose purpose is unknown to us.

The Gymnasium

Between the two sanctuaries, archaeologists have uncovered the **Gymnasium** of Delphi, which was built in around 330 BC on two flat areas. All along the upper level was the *xystos*, a colonnade in which the athletes could train under cover, with 83 columns on its facade. In front of the *xystos* was the open track or *paradromis*. On the lower level was the *palaestra*, or wrestling ground, with colonnades around a square court. To the north-west, a circular **cistern** which stored water for the athletes to bathe in has been found, along with **Roman baths**. In 1743, a little monastery dedicated to Our Lady occupied the site of the *palaestra*.

The Castalian Spring

Above the stadium towered the cliffs called the Phaedriades, in which was the ancient **Castalian spring**. The water ran down to a fountain of the seventh or sixth century BC close to the modern main road. Behind, higher up on the rocks, can be seen the ruins of another fountain, of the Roman period. It was in the Castalian spring that the Pythia washed, as did visitors to Delphi, thus taking in some of the prophetic properties of the water.

DELPHI MUSEUM

Next to the archaeological site at Delphi is one of the most important **museums** in all Greece, devoted exclusively to finds from the surrounding area.

In the **entrance hall** is a 'navel-stone' of the Roman period, together with sections of a frieze showing scenes from the feats of Heracles, added to the proscenium of the theatre in the first century BC. **Room 1** contains copper votive offerings of the seventh century BC. **Room 2** is dominated by the sculptures which once ornamented the treasury of the Siphnians (525 BC). The frieze depicted scenes from the Trojan War (east side), the Battle of the Giants (north side), the Judgement of Paris (west side) and the Rape of the Daughters of Leucippus (south side). One of the pediments bore the dispute between Heracles and Apollo over the Delphic tripod. One of the two Caryatids on the facade and sections of the relief of the door frame have also survived. Also in this room are the Sphinx of the Naxians (560 BC), a Caryatid from the treasury of Cnidus (550-545 BC), and a column capital in the Aeolic order from the treasury of Massalia (500 BC). The most striking exhibits in **Room 3** are two colossal statues of the early sixth century BC representing the Argive heroes Cleobis and

p. 72

Above: part of the north frieze of the Treasury of the Siphnians, showing a scene from the Battle of the Giants (525 BC, room 2).

Left: statue of Antinoos, favourite of the Emperor Hadrian, who was deified after he drowned himself in the river Nile (room 12).

◄ p. 73

Metope from the Treasury of the Athenians: Heracles and the Hind of Ceryneia (sixth century BC, room 5).

pp. 74-75

Part of the north frieze of the Treasury of the Siphnians, showing a scene from the Battle of the Giants (525 BC, room 2).

p. 75

A huge head, probably from a gold and ivory statue of Apollo (550 BC, room 4).

Biton, together with metopes from the simple building of 560 BC over which the treasury of Sikyon was built (the voyage of the *Argo*, the Rape of Europa, the hunting of the Calydonian boar, Phrixus with the Golden Fleece). **Room 4** is largely given over to metal objects found buried in the Halos (8th-5th century BC): an enormous silver bull, bronze statuettes, and fragments of three impressive chryselephantine statues which probably represented Apollo, Leto and Artemis. **Room 5** is adorned with the metopes from the treasury of the Athenians, with scenes from the exploits of Heracles and Theseus (6th century BC). In **Room 6** are statues, two hymns to Apollo preserving musical notation (2nd century BC), and the sculptures from the west pediment of the temple of Apollo (that erected by the Alcmaeonids): a Battle of the Giants by the sculptor Antenor. The east pediment of the building is on display in **Room 7**, and shows the emergence of Apollo on his chariot. A statue of Dionysus which would have been fixed to the west pediment of the fourth-century temple has also survived. Funerary *stelae*, terracotta busts, vases dating from the Classical period and statues are among the exhibits in **Room 8**, while the most striking objects on view in **Room 9** are the sculptures from the frieze of the Tholos in the sanctuary of Athena Pronaea (400-390 BC), with scenes from the Battle of the Centaurs and the Battle of the Giants. **Room 10** contains a reconstruction of the monument of Daochus II, including statues of the king and his family and of Apollo (330 BC). The most famous exhibit in the museum is to be seen in **Room 11**: this is the bronze statue of the Charioteer, from a group also containing the chariot and horses dedicated by Polyzalus to mark his victory in the

Pythian Games of 474 BC. This is one of the most impressive sculptures of the 'severe style', and some scholars attribute it to the sculptor Pythagoras. In **Room 12** we note the Roman statue of Antinous, the pottery from the Corycian Cave on Mt Parnassus (7th-4th centuries BC), and the prehistoric finds from the cemeteries of Delphi and from Crisa.

ARACHOVA

Not far from the archaeological site is the modern village of Delphi, occupying a position of the greatest beauty, while 12 kilometres to the east is **Arachova**, at an altitude of 960 metres. The town is a busy tourist resort, especially in the winter months because of the nearby winter sports centre on Mt Parnassus. Arachova is well-known for its woven goods and other handicrafts.

NAUPACTUS
(NAFPAKTOS)

In antiquity, the city of Naupactus on the Gulf of Corinth belonged to the Ozolian Locrians. Later it became the capital of Aetolia and was an important political and military centre in the Aeolian League. In 146 BC, it was conquered by the Romans, and under Byzantium it was the seat of a bishop. In 1210, Naupactus was incorporated into the Despotate of Epirus, and in 1403 it was sold to the Venetians. In 1499 the Turks took it, and their occupation lasted until 1829 with a brief period of Venetian rule from 1687 to 1700. Naupactus was the scene, in 1571, of the Battle of Lepanto between the Turks and the united fleets of Venice, Spain and Pope Pius V. The defeat of the Ottoman Empire in that battle marked the beginning of the collapse of its sea power.

Modern Nafpaktos is a tourist resort with many interesting sights, including the fine **Venetian castle**, which has survived in quite good condition, and the harbour with its Venetian towers and bastions.

p. 76
View of the harbour at Nafpaktos, with the Venetian towers. In the background, the Venetian castle rises above the pretty town.

MESOLONGI

Mesolongi is the chief town of the Prefecture of Aitoloakarnania. The region known as Aetolia, of which Mesolongi is part, was inhabited in prehistoric times. In the time of Philip II, the Aetolians emerged as a strong political force, and in the third century BC they formed the Aetolian League, which was an important focus for resistance against the spreading power of Rome.

Mesolongi was particularly prosperous during the seventeenth and eighteenth centuries, developing into the commercial and maritime centre of Central Greece. During the Greek War of Independence, the townspeople won great fame for their bravery and heroism. Mesolongi had thrown itself into the struggle as soon as the War of Independence broke out, and it received valuable support from Lord Byron, who died in the town in 1824. Perhaps, though, the greatest acts of heroism in Mesolongi are those associated with the siege of the town by the Turks. There were two sieges, in 1822 and 1825; on the second occasion, the water and food ran out altogether, and on 12 April 1826 the townspeople decided to break out, although they knew that the numerical superiority of the Turks was such that not all of them would escape. Their decision to risk death rather than surrender made the Mesolongi breakout a symbol of the entire War of Independence. Today, there are many monuments in the town connected with the breakout: the **Breakout Gate**, **monuments** to the leaders of the Greeks and to the Philhellenes who fought by their side, and a **Museum** with manuscripts, paintings, maps and documents. The heroism of the people of Mesolongi has also inspired painters and poets from all over the world.

Mesolongi is known for its **lagoon**; it and the similar lagoon at nearby Aitoliko are among the largest wetlands in Europe. From the point of view of tourist interest, the most fascinating features of the lagoon are the narrow strips of land which separate it from the open sea, and the lake-dwellings made of wood, reeds and water-resistant vegetation, standing on piles in the lake.

THERMOPYLAE

The **pass of Thermopylae** separates Mt Kallidromo from the sea of the Malliakos Gulf. One kilometre long and - in antiquity - only 5-20 metres broad, the pass was the scene of many battles down the centuries, the most famous of them being the heroic resistance of the Spartans to the invading Persians in 480 BC. Xerxes, the Persian king, had brought his enormous army west and south through northern Greece, but the Greeks were waiting for him at Thermopylae. The Greek forces resisted bravely, but were betrayed by a certain Ephialtes, who showed the Persians how to outflank the Greeks along a mountain path called the Anopaea. The Spartan general Leonidas now held the battlefield with 300 of his own people and 700 men of Thespiae - all of whom fought to the death, after first killing large numbers of Persians. There is a statue of Leonidas on the battlefield now, to commemorate the heroism of the Spartans.

p. 77

The statue of Leonidas now standing at the Pass of Thermopylae to commemorate the heroic resistance of the Spartans to the Persian invasion.

EUBOEA (EVVIA)

pp. 78-79
Below: views of Chalkida with the bridge over the Evripos channel.

p. 79
Above: view of the archaeological site of Eretria. In the background, the modern town.

Euboea is really more of an extension of Central Greece than an island, since a bridge only a few hundred metres long over the tidal Euripus channel separates it from Attica. To the east, Euboea is washed by the Aegean Sea, while to the west the Euripus divides the channel into the North and South Euboean Gulfs.

Euboea was first inhabited in Neolithic times, and in the seventh century BC was colonised by the Ionians who had also been active in building cities in Macedonia, Sicily and Italy. In the late sixth century, Euboea was conquered by Athens and its land was divided up among Athenian settlers. After the fourth century BC, the island was occupied by the Thebans (371 BC), the Macedonians (349 BC) and the Romans (194 BC). After many centuries of Byzantine rule, Frankish overlords took it in 1204. In 1366, the Venetians renamed the island Negroponte. The Ottoman occupation lasted from 1470 to 1829.

The chief town of Euboea is **Chalkida**, which as ancient Chalcis was an important naval power and founded many colonies, especially in Chalcidice. To the east of the modern town are traces of its ancient forerunner, and interesting finds from the site are to be seen in the small **Archaeological**

Museum. **Eretria** was also a strong city in antiquity, and the constant rival of Chalcis. There are fascinating remains of the ancient city to be seen today near the modern town of the same name: **walls, a temple of Apollo Daphnophorus, a temple of Dionysus, a theatre**, parts of the **harbour, the gymnasium,** and **Roman houses** with mosaics.

Apart from these two cities, Euboea can boast many towns and villages of interest to visitors. Among the island's advantages is the constantly varying landscape as one moves from north to south, indicative of the potential of Euboea for winter tourism as well as summer holidays.

THE PELOPONNESE

pp. 80-81

Above: Epidaurus theatre.
Facing page (large photograph): Monemvasia.

Below: corner antefix from a building at Olympia (430 BC, Olympia Museum).

The Peloponnese, southernmost part of the Balkan peninsula, is the largest peninsula in Greece, with an area of 21,439 square kilometres. It is linked to central Greece across an isthmus at whose narrowest point (6 km.) the Corinth Canal was constructed in 1892. The Peloponnese is washed by the Aegean, and its coastlines form the Saronic and Argolic Gulfs to the east, the Gulfs of Laconia and Messenia to the south, the Gulf of Kyparissia to the west, and the Gulfs of Patra and Corinth to the north. The terrain is largely mountainous, with Mt Taygetus, in the south, the highest peak at 2407 m. Among other important mountains are the Yeraneia range (1351 m.), Arachnaio (1199 m.), Kyllini (2376 m.), Aroania (2340 m.), Erymanthos (2224 m.), Panachaiko (1926 m.), Maenalo (1980 m.) and Parnon (1939 m.). Flatter areas are confined to the coasts and the valleys of the rivers (Asopos, Vouraikos, Peneios, Alpheios, Nedas, Evrotas, Nedon and Pamisos). The climate is Mediterranean, but there is much variation from place to place, making possible a wide range of crops (cereals, citrus fruit, vines, tobacco, olives and vegetables). The modern administrative division into seven prefectures reflects the organisation of ancient times.

p. 82

A wall-painting of the thirteenth century BC from the Mycenean palace at Tiryns (National Archaeological Museum, Athens).

p. 83

The temple of Hera at Olympia: girls in ancient costume are preparing to light the Olympic Flame at the ceremony which marks the beginning of the Olympic Games period.

The Peloponnese (literally, 'island of Pelops') takes its name from Pelops, a mythical hero who was a descendant of Tantalus. According to the tradition, Pelops succeeded in gaining control over the area when he defeated King Oenomaus of Pisa, a city in Eleia, in a chariot race and won the hand in marriage of Oenomaus' daughter Hippodameia. In one version of the myth, this was how the Olympic Games began. The royal lines of the Pelopids and Atreides, descendants of Pelops, then ruled at Mycenae and Sparta.

The oldest human settlements in the Peloponnese date back to the Neolithic period, with the presence of the first Greeks confirmed as having begun around 2000 BC. It was these new colonists, of the tribe of the Achaeans, who were responsible for the cultural development that occurred in the next few centuries and led to the emergence of the Mycenean civilisation. The Achaeans were great merchants and seamen, and after absorbing much of importance from the Minoans of Crete, who had ruled the seas down to that time, they succeeded in outstripping their rivals and in commanding the entire Aegean. Towards the end of the fourteenth century BC, the cities of Mycenae, Tiryns, Argos and Pylos reached the height of their power and wealth, as we can see in the archaeological finds from their sites. The centres of Mycenean power then went into decline and were destroyed in the late twelfth century BC, for reasons which are still not fully understood.

At about this time, a new tribe, the Dorians, flooded south into the Peloponnese and conquered Corinthia, the Argolid, Laconia and Messenia, consolidating their power during the ninth and eighth centuries. The centre of Doric power was at Sparta, which in a series of wars (the Messenian Wars) subdued Messenia on the other side of Mt Taygetus. Most of the cities of the Peloponnese were active in the founding of colonies, usually in Lower Italy and Sicily, though also elsewhere: Corfu, for instance, was Corinthian.

A similar policy of expansion was kept up through the seventh and sixth centuries BC, with significant parallel development in commerce, shipping and industry. Most of the cities were ruled by tyrants. Sparta soon emerged as the most powerful city-state in the Peloponnese, gaining influence which enabled it to impose its own aristocratic regime even on far-away Athens (for a short period after 508 BC). In the early fifth century, the cities of the Peloponnese - except for Argos and Achaea - participated actively in the Persian Wars. Sparta led the Greek land forces in the battles of Thermopylae, Salamis, Plataeae and Mycale (480/479 BC). But the constantly growing power of Sparta led to conflict with Athens; in 431 BC, after a

series of minor clashes, the Peloponnesian War broke out, ending in 404 BC with the total defeat of Athens. For a period, Sparta was the ruling power in the whole of Greece, but she was unable to prevent the expansion of Thebes, which - on the initiative of Epaminondas - founded Megalopolis and Messene, on the Spartan borders, in 370/369 BC. In the meantime, Philip II of Macedon was extending his influence over the whole of Greece, and in 342 was recognised by an assembly of Greek cities at Corinth as commander of the Greek forces in the forthcoming operations against the Persians. Despite Peloponnesian opposition, this post passed to his son Alexander. The death of Alexander was followed by civil war, and in 303 BC most of the city-states of the Peloponnese were conquered by Demetrius Poliorcetes. In 280 BC the Achaean League was founded; although this succeeded in keeping the Macedonians at bay, it was unable to deal with the Romans, who eventually captured the entire Peloponnese in 146 BC. Under the Romans, the Peloponnese was part of the Province of Achaea, the commander of which had his headquarters at Corinth. In the third and fourth centuries AD, the Peloponnese was ravaged by raiding Goths and by Alaric. From the seventh to the eleventh centuries, Corinth was the capital of the Byzantine *theme* of the Peloponnese, and later of the *theme* of Greece.

In 1204, after the capture of Constantinople by the 'Franks', William de Champlit and Geoffrey I Villehardouin founded the Principality of the Morea,

p. 84
View of Megalou Spilaiou Monastery near Kalavryta. The buildings rise to a height of eight storeys against the steep sides of Mt Chelmos.

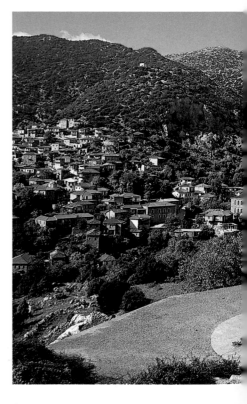

which consisted of the entire peninsula with the exception of Argos, Nauplion, Methone, Corone and Monemvasia. In 1262, after his defeat at the Battle of Pelagonia, William II Villehardouin was compelled to surrender the fortresses of the Peloponnese to the Byzantine Emperor, Michael VIII Palaeologus, and this marked the beginning of the end for the Frankish principality. The Byzantines went on to found the Despotate of the Morea, whose capital was at Mystras, a city which developed into the centre of Byzantine culture in the area.

In 1458-1460, Mohammed II succeeded in taking the Peloponnese for the Ottoman Empire, thus bringing to a close a campaign which had started in the time of Constantine Palaeologus and Murat II (1446). The expansion of Turkish power was a threat to Venice, which embarked upon a series of military operations - the Turkish-Venetian Wars - to protect its territories. In 1684, the entire Peloponnese was controlled by Francesco Morosini, the Venetian commander, but by 1714 it was back in Turkish hands. The Peloponnese played a leading role in the War of Independence of 1821. The Struggle began in Achaea and the Mani, its conventional date of commencement being taken to be the reading of a proclamation in Ayiou Yeorgiou Square in Patra by the local bishop, Germanos, on 25 March 1821. In 1830, the independence of modern Greece - then consisting only of the Peloponnese, southern Central Greece and the Cyclades - obtained international recognition.

p. 84 - 85
Stemnitsa

THE ISTHMUS OF CORINTH - THE DIOLCUS

The Corinth Canal, with a length of 6 kilometres and a width of 23 metres, was constructed between 1882 and 1893 by French and Greek engineers at the narrowest point of the isthmus. This impressive work of engineering, which we cross by a bridge as we leave Attica and enter the Peloponnese, joined the Corinthian and Saronic Gulfs. Ships sailing from Piraeus towards the Adriatic no longer needed to sail right round the Peloponnese, thus shortening the voyage by 185 nautical miles. The decision to build a canal in this spot had been taken many times in antiquity - by Periander, tyrant of Corinth, by Demetrius Poliorcetes, by Julius Caesar, by Nero,

by Hadrian and by Herodes Atticus - and in 67 AD Nero went so far as to inaugurate the project by cutting the first sod with a golden pick. But it was not until the nineteenth century that the canal was actually completed.

Nonetheless, the ancient Greeks had devised another means of solving the problem of communication between the two gulfs. In the late seventh or early sixth century, they constructed a paved road called the *diolcus* from the shores of the Saronic Gulf to those of the Corinthian, and ships were pulled on wheeled wagons from one piece of sea to the other. Parts of the *diolcus* can still be seen today, at the end of the canal on the Gulf of Corinth.

ISTHMIA

The area known as Isthmia lies to the south-east of the Corinth Canal. Near the village of Kyravrysi are the ruins of the famous **sanctuary of Poseidon**. Poseidon was the god in whose honour the Isthmian Games - reorganised in 582 on the lines of the Olympic Games and held in the sanctuary every two years - took place. According to tradition, the Games were instituted to honour Melicertes-Palaemon. Melicertes was the illegitimate son of Athamas, king of Boeotia, by Ino. Athamas already had three children - Phrixus, Glaucon and Helle - by his rightful wife, Nephele, and Ino plotted the deaths of these offspring. The goddess Hera decided to punish Ino, and chased her as far as the Saronic Gulf, where she drowned with her son Melicertes. Zeus then deified them both, changing their names to Leucothea and Palaemon. The dead

p. 86
The Saronic Gulf end of the Corinth Canal.

p. 87
View of the impressive Corinth Canal, which links the Gulf of Corinth and the Saronic Gulf.

boy was brought to shore by a dolphin, and later worshipped as a local hero. According to another version of the story, the Isthmian Games were initially founded by the Athenian hero Theseus in honour of Poseidon.

In the archaeological site of Isthmia, we can see the foundations of the fourth-century **temple of Poseidon**. The earliest temple on this site was built in the first half of the seventh century BC. It had wooden columns, and was unusually elongated. Its saddle-back roof covered the cult statues of Poseidon and Amphitrite. Somewhere around 470-460 BC, this Archaic temple was burned down, and immediately rebuilt along the lines of the temple of Zeus at Olympia (peripteral and in the Doric order). In 390 BC the temple was once more destroyed by fire, and soon replaced by another in the same style. In the Roman period, a precinct was constructed round the temple, later being extended and reinforced with Ionic colonnades on its inner side and a monumental propylum in the southeast corner.

In the first century AD, a sanctuary in honour of Melicertes-Palaemon was built to the south of the temple. Inside a precinct, the circular temple on a raised platform had at its centre a statue of a dolphin with Palaemon on its back. The **Palaemonium** also had an underground crypt in which mystical ceremonies were held at night.

The site of the Palaemonium was once occupied by the Classical **stadium** of Isthmia, which at the end of the fourth century BC was moved further to the south; traces of it can be detected on the hill called Rachi. Of the earlier structure, all that has survived is the *apheteria* or starter's box, with its triangular limestone floor. At one corner of the triangle is a pit one metre deep, in which the starter stood in order to ensure that the runners set off together.

Approximately 30 m. to the south of the temple of Poseidon, archaeologists have discovered the **theatre** of Isthmia, which was built in the Classical period and reconstructed on a number of occasions before the end of Roman rule.

Almost all of the masonry from the theatre, the temple and the other buildings in the sanctuary was used in the construction of the *Hexamilio*, or **Isthmian Wall**, under Justinian (6th century AD). The Wall, 7,300 metres in length, followed the line of earlier fortifications and underwent frequent repairs during the Byzantine period. Some sections of it are still visible today between the Corinthian and Saronic Gulfs. Next to the archaeological site is a **Museum**, with finds from the sanctuary and from Cenchreae. In the **entrance hall** are stone pillars concerning the Isthmian Games, with seventh-century BC architectural members from the temple of Poseidon. The **main room** is divided into two sections; in the first, with exhibits from Isthmia, we will note the pottery dating from prehistoric to Roman times and the votive offerings from the sanctuary of Poseidon. In the second, there are finds from **Cenchreae**, Corinth's port on the Saronic Gulf. Apart from the pottery, the wooden items and the ivories, there is also a particularly interesting series of glass panels in the *opus sectile* technique, involving the use of mosaics in a variety of colours. These 87 panels were found packed in crates just as they had been brought to Cenchreae when a disastrous earthquake, in 375 AD, prevented them from ever being delivered.

p. 88

View of the archaeological site at Isthmia, where the Isthmian Games were held in honour of the god Poseidon.

CORINTH (KORINTHOS)

p. 90

Above: wooden tablet from Pitsa in Corinthia, showing a sacrifice (540 BC, National Arch. Museum, Athens).

Below: a Corinthian alabaster vase with painted ornamentation (600 BC, Corinth Museum).

Corinth was inhabited for the first time in the Neolithic period, somewhere round about the end of the fifth millenium BC. This was a good site for human settlement, because there was plenty of water and the terrain was ideal, with the rock of the Acrocorinth towering to the south - a natural fortress which soon became the acropolis of the city - the harbours of the Lechaeum and Cenchreae close at hand, and nearby the isthmus, the only land bridge between the Peloponnese and Central Greece. In prehistoric times, Corinth was one of the richest cities of the Greek world. The first semi-historical king whose name we know was Aletes, leader of the Dorians, who arrived here in around 1000-900 BC. In the eighth century BC, thanks to the wise government of the Bacchiadae dynasty, Corinth was able to found the colonies of Corfu and Syracuse, and developed into the leading naval power in Greece. In 657 BC, Cypselus, with the support of the people, established a tyrannical regime. He and his son Periander - one of the Seven Sages of the ancient world - founded still more colonies, supported the arts and sciences and reorganised the Isthmian Games. In 580 BC, the Cypselid tyranny was overthrown by Sparta, and the aristocratic faction was strengthened. At this time, Corinth became an ally of Sparta and one of the most powerful members of the Peloponnesian League. During the Persian Wars, Corinth took part in almost all the battles; later, when the question of how to

◄ *p. 91*

*View of ancient
Corinth.*

deal with Athenian power arose, the city was one of the instigators of the Peloponnesian War. Despite its loyalty to victorious Sparta, it nonetheless discovered when the fighting was over that much of its power was gone. Thus it allied itself with other city-states and turned on Sparta, provoking the Corinthian War of 395-387 BC. In 338 BC, Corinth was taken by Philip II of Macedon, who at Isthmia in the same year was appointed commander-in-chief of the Greek forces and, effectively, king of Greece. Alexander the

Great called a conference, also at Isthmia, which confirmed his succession to these posts for the campaign against Persia. In 243 BC, Corinth joined the Achaean League and emerged as its chief city. But the forces of Achaea were overcome by the Roman general Leucius Mommius, who in 146 BC looted and devastated Corinth. It was not until a century later that its reconstruction was ordered by Julius Caesar. In the first century AD, Corinth was the capital of the Roman province of Achaea, and in the second century it was

endowed with fine buildings by the Emperor Hadrian and by Herodes Atticus. Between the Byzantine period and the nineteenth century, Corinth was frequently raided and invaded: by the Heruli, the Goths, the Normans, the Crusaders, the Franks, the Venetians and, in 1459, the Turks. It was liberated immediately after the outbreak of the War of Independence in 1821 and laid claim, unsuccessfully, to the right to be capital of the new state. In 1858, Corinth was flattened by a major earthquake and moved to a new site closer to the Isthmus. This new city was again struck by earthquake, and rebuilt in 1929.

The remains of ancient Corinth - as rebuilt by Julius Caesar in 44 BC - lie not far from the modern city. The archaeological site contains a **Roman Forum** built in the same position as the ancient Agora. At the west entrance to the archaeological site (there is another entrance to the north) is **Temple E**, of the first century AD, dedicated - according to most scholars - to Octavia, sister of Octavian. The temple stands on a

p. 92 - 93

Views of ancient Corinth.

podium, in line with the Roman approach to architecture, and was in the Corinthian order.

To the east of Temple E was a road running along a north-south axis which led to Sikyon. Beside it are the **west shops**, of the first century AD, and the Roman **temple of Hera Acraea**, whose cult had established itself in the area in the Greek era. Behind the temple of Hera, the **spring of Glauce** had been carved out of the rock as far back as the sixth century BC. On the east side of the Sikyon road, on a piece of higher ground, stand the seven surviving columns of the **temple of Apollo**. This imposing structure was built around 540 BC to replace an earlier temple of the seventh century. It is one of the earliest, yet most characteristic, Doric peripteral temples, with unusually heavy and elongated proportions.

To the north of the temple of Apollo was the **North Forum** of Imperial times, and to its south was the **north stoa**. This stoa was built in the third century BC, with Doric columns on its facade and Ionic columns inside. In the first century AD, the Romans built walls in the gaps between the columns and turned the stoa into a storehouse. In front, they erected shops with vaulted roofs. In the vicinity of the north shops was an **underground vaulted temple,** of the sixth century BC, where according to tradition oracles were given and miracles performed. The temple was connected with a **sacred spring**, from which a frieze has survived.

The west side of the forum was occupied by a line of six small Roman temples on a podium: the Ionic **temple of Fortuna and Venus**, the **Pantheon** in the Corinthian order, two **temples** probably dedicated to **Heracles and Poseidon**, the single-winged circular **temple of Apollo Clarius** and a **temple of Hermes**.

In the market square *per se* were the **central shops** on either side of the **bema** or rostrum from which the Corinthians could be addressed. It was to this rostrum that St Paul was led to be tried by Gallius, the Roman governor, when the Apostle visited Corinth in 51 AD. An **early Christian basilica** was later constructed on the site.

On the south side of the market square, the **south stoa** was built in the fourth century BC. This was one of the largest buildings anywhere in Greece, boasting 71 Doric columns on its exterior and 34 Ionic columns inside. The shops in the stoa seem to have been used as taverns. The Romans reconstructed the building and added a number of administrative offices: the **office of the agonothetes**, the luxurious **office of the commander of the province of Achaea**, and the **bouleuterium** or Curia. Behind the Curia, a road set off for the harbour at Cenchreae.

A number of Roman basilicas, buildings used for administrative purposes, have come to light in the Forum at Corinth. The most important of these is the **Julian Basilica**, on the east of the market square. It was built in the time of Augustus, and was ornamented with statues of the imperial family. The **starting-line of the Classical stadium** of Corinth, which lay beneath the market square, has been excavated by the facade of this multistorey building. The stadium was the scene of the Hellotia, a festival in honour of the dead.

Half-way along the north side of the Forum was the ancient entrance to the area, which coincides with the second modern entrance. In the first century BC, a monumental **propylum** was constructed there, consisting of a marble triumphal arch supporting bronze statues of Helius and Phaeton. The propylum marked the end of the paved Lechaean Way, which started at the port of Lechaeum and was flanked by important buildings. On the west side of the Lechaean Way was a Classical stoa which in Roman times was replaced by the **north basilica**. On the Forum side, the facade of the basilica had two storeys ornamented with **statues of barbarian prisoners** (3rd century AD). To the east of the Lechaean Way, the famous **Peirene Fountain** had been built in Classical times. In the second century AD, Herodes Atticus rebuilt the structure, making it more elaborate. The new fountain had two storeys and was richly ornamented with recesses, statues and wall-paintings. To the north of the fountain, the foundations have survived of the **precinct of Apollo** (1st century AD), on the west of which a small fourth-century temple once stood. To the north, archaeologists have explored the **baths of Eurycles**, built in the first century AD on the site of fifth-century baths.

This area has also yielded the ruins of a Roman **Odeum** of the first century AD, which Herodes Atticus reconstructed in the second century AD and which had become an arena for fights

p. 95

The north shops of ancient Corinth, with the temple of Apollo in the background.

with wild beasts by 225 AD. Near the Odeum was the **theatre**, of the first century AD, on the site of the fifth-century Classical theatre.

Corinth also had a sanctuary of the healer-god Asclepius, traces of which can be seen to the north of the theatre. The **Asclepium** of Corinth dates from the sixth century BC, with the god's temple being constructed in the fourth century BC.

At the north entrance to the archaeological site is the **Museum**, which contains highly important finds from the site. The room **to the right of the entrance** shows the pottery produced in Corinth in the Archaic perid, when microscopic containers (for scent, wine or other commodities) made in the city were exported all over the Mediterranean and displaced the pottery of Attica. There are also examples of black-figure ware, terracotta statuettes, two Archaic funerary sphinxes, the torso of a *kore* dating from the early fifth century BC, and vases of the Classical period. The **room to the left of the entrance** is occupied by important sculptures of the Roman period: statues of Roman leaders, the statues of the family of Augustus from the Julian Basilica, and the colossal figures of the barbarians from the facade of the prisoners in the Forum of Corinth. There are also striking Roman mosaics, of the highest quality, with plant motifs, depictions of landscapes and mythical themes. On display, too, are relief slabs with mythological scenes from the theatre of Corinth (2nd century AD). In a **separate room** are the finds from the sanctuary of Asclepius, chiefly consisting of terracotta replicas of cured members offered to the sanctuary by grateful patients.

ACROCORINTH

To the south-west of ancient Corinth towers the imposing bulk of the Acrocorinth (575 m. in height), after the Acropolis of Athens the earliest inhabited place in Greece to have been continuously occupied. In ancient times, it was the acropolis of Corinth, and as early as the Archaic period it was sealed off by a **precinct** of its own within the city walls. Today, some sections of the

fourth-century fortifications have survived, along with defensive works of the Roman period and the Middle Ages. The Acrocorinth was the site of the cult of **Aphrodite**, of whose **temple** a few scattered traces on the topmost peak of the rock have survived. According to tradition, the cult of the goddess was practised by priestesses who were also courtesans, their latter capacity allowing them to earn considerable sums of money for the sanctuary. Up on the hill there was also a **sanctuary of the sun god Helius**: there was a myth to the effect that Helius and Poseidon had disputed over which was to be the patron of the Acrocorinth and the Isthmus, and had decided to share them. Near the temple of Aphrodite was the **Upper Peirene spring**, dedicated, like its counterpart in the Forum, to the mythical Peirene, mother of Cenchrias and Lechaeus.

In the medieval period, the Acrocorinth had many masters. In 1210 it was captured by Otto de la Roche, prince of Athens, and Geoffrey I

pp. 96-97
The Doric temple of Apollo at ancient Corinth, 540 BC.

Villehardouin. In the mid-thirteenth century, William Villehardouin extended the fortifications, and so did Jean Gravin, prince of the Angevins, in the fourteenth century. In 1358, Niccolo Acciajuoli took the area, followed in 1394 by Theodore I Palaeologus, Despot of Mystras. After a brief period of occupation by the Knights of the Order of St John, the castle was taken in 1458 by the Turks, who held it until 1821 with the exception of a spell of Venetian possession in 1687-1715. The line of the walls has remained almost the same since Classical times, consisting of three zones of fortifications with a gate in each. From the summit of the Acrocorinth there is a stunning view across the Peloponnese and north to Mt Parnassus.

p. 98
Red-figure
amphora showing
Heracles and the
Stymphalian
Birds (500 BC,
the Louvre).

p. 99
Right: the
surviving
columns of the
temple of Zeus
at Nemea,
330-320 BC.

STYMPHALIA - NEMEA

Stymphalia, 40 km. to the south of Kiato on the Gulf of Corinth, is associated with one of the Labours of Heracles: according to the tradition, it was here, on the shores of the lake, that the hero killed the Birds of Stymphalia which had been plaguing the surrounding area.

Another of the Labours was accomplished at **Nemea**, on the border between Corinthia and the Argolid. There, Heracles killed a fierce lion which had been terrorising the countrypeople. Nemea's main claim to fame, however, was the Nemean Games, held in honour of Zeus every two years under the supervision first of the city of Cleonae and later of Argos. The Nemean Games were traditionally supposed to have been instituted in memory of Opheltes, son of the local king, who was unlucky enough to be killed by a poisonous snake when his nurse left him alone by a spring. So it came about that the Nemean Games, like three of the other Panhellenic festivals, were founded in order to commemorate a dead hero and were originally funeral games. They were reorganised in 573 BC and consisted of athletic contests whose winners received wreaths of wild celery as prizes.

At the archaeological site, we can see the **stadium**, built in the late fourth century BC. It was in the shape of a horseshoe and had seating for the spectators hewn out of the rock.

Very close to the Stadium was the **sanctuary of Zeus**, where a temple to the god was first erected in the Archaic period. In 330-320 BC, a new temple, in the Doric order and peripteral in design, was built; it is usually regarded as marking the end of the Classical Doric order, since rather than adopting the usual Classical tendency to develop the temple with equal sides around its centre, this building has much broader proportions and an accentuated facade. Inside the temple was an *adyton* where the tomb of Opheltes was located.

Nemea has a little **museum** with architectural members from the temple of Zeus and the buildings in the surrounding area, silver and copper coins, artefacts connected with the Games, items associated with the cult of Opheltes, prehistoric finds from the vicinity of Nemea and pottery of the Roman and Byzantine periods.

p. 100

Above: wall-painting of the thirteenth-century from the acropolis of Mycenae (National Arch. Museum, Athens).

Below: head of a gold pin from Mycenae (second half of the sixteenth century BC, National Arch. Museum, Athens).

MYCENAE (MYKINES)

The name of Mycenae is associated with the most important of the Greek cycles of myths, as it has come down to us in the epics of Homer and in the works of the great tragedians of antiquity. According to the story, Mycenae was founded by Perseus, son of Zeus and Danae, and his descendants ruled in the area for many generations. The Perseid clan was succeeded by the dynasty of the Atreids, founded by Atreus, son of Pelops and Hippodamia. The son of Atreus was Agamemnon, proud leader of the Greeks during the campaign against Troy. On his return to Mycenae after the victorious conclusion to the Trojan War, Agamemnon was murdered by his wife Clytemnestra and her lover Aegisthus. His son and daughter, Orestes and Electra, then killed Clytemnestra and Aegisthus and were avenged for the death of Agamemnon. According to most scholars, the ruin of Mycenae came about during the reign of Tisamenus, son of Orestes. The mythological background to the history of Mycenae was borne out by the excavations begun on the site by the Greek Archaeological Association (1841) and Heinrich Schliemann (1876) and continued by C. Tsoundas (1880-1902), A. Wace (to 1957), I. Papadimitriou, Y. Mylonas (1952-1955) and Lord Taylour. The hill of Mycenae, 278 metres high, is separated by precipitous gorges from the steep slopes of Mt Profitis Ilias and Mt Sara. Human habitation on the hill dates back to

Neolithic times, but it was not until the Late Helladic period (1600-1100 BC) that Mycenae gained in power and prestige, ultimately giving its name to an entire historical period. Around 1100 BC, the city was utterly devastated and the acropolis passed into the hands of Argos. The Argives demolished the walls in 468 BC, but in the third century BC they refounded a fortified city on the site. This, in turn, seems to have decline and become deserted in Roman times, for the traveller Pausanias, in the second century AD, found only ruins at Mycenae.

In the centuries of its greatest power, Mycenae was the centre of the Mycenean civilisation. It stood on an acropolis surrounded by **walls** which were as much as 12 metres high. Huge undressed boulders were used to build these walls, although more care was taken with the blocks near the Lion Gate. The imposing appearance of these walls was explained by a tradition that they had been constructed by the Cyclopes, giants from Lycia in Asia Minor (Cyclopean Walls). The acropolis was first fortified around 1350 BC, and the walls were extended in the mid-thirteenth century to enclose Grave Circle A. It was at this time that the Lion Gate and the North Gate were built. Late in the thirteenth century, the wall was extended north-east so as to protect the underground water cistern constructed there. The walls, in the sedimentary rock called breccia,

◄ p. 101
The famous Lion Gate at Mycenae, thirteenth century BC.

p. 102
Part of the 'Cyclopean' walls flanking the Lion Gate.

have always been visible down the centuries, and the place where the blocks of stone were quarried has been identified near Mycenae.

The **Lion Gate**, on the north-west side of the acropolis, is to be seen today in its original form, with the exception of the top two blocks of stone on the right. In front of the Gate was an outer courtyard, bounded on the west by a tower - a new element in the art of fortification and one which improved the defences of the Gate. The step, gateposts and lintel (weighing 18 tons) are all single blocks of stone: four of them altogether. As in the case of the *tholos* tombs, there was a relieving triangle above the gate, with a slab of grey limetone in it. On the slab are depicted two lions, facing each other, with two joined altars and a Minoan pillar. The superb lion relief is admired by the thousands of visitors to the site each year, and has been interpreted in a variety of ways: as purely ornamental, as the emblem of the kings of Mycenae, as a sacred symbol, as an indication of Egyptian influence, or as evidence of the link between Mycenae and Minoan Crete. Whatever its meaning or origin, it is a superb work of art, combining symmetry of form with the fierceness in the depiction of the lions. On the inner side of the gate - which had a double door - was a second courtyard, probably roofed in.

On the right of this courtyard was the **Granary**, so-called because of the

p. 103
The hill of Mycenae and the fortified acropolis. In the background, Mt Profitis Ilias.

storage jars of carbonised wheat and the twelfth-century vases found there (in the so-called 'Granary order'). Further to the south, Schliemann discovered **Grave Circle A**, whose nineteen occupants had been interred with gold artefacts to a total weight of 14 kilos. The quantity of gold confirmed Homer in his description of Mycenae as "rich in gold", but it also raised a question which is still unanswered: where did all this wealth - now on display in the Archaeological Museum in Athens - come from? Grave Circle A consists of a double ring of slabs constructed in the mid-thirteenth century BC, but the burials it contains, all of them undoubtedly royal, date from the mid-sixteenth century. The Myceneans seem to have taken particular care to protect the tombs of their former leaders, which they enclosed in a wall. A total of six shaft graves were discovered, consisting of simple pits dug into the rock and covered by heaps of soil on which stone funerary *stelae* were then erected. The 17 *stelae* recovered are decorated, in low relief, with spirals and scenes from the hunt, battle and chariot-racing.

To the south east of Grave Circle A was a series of houses and shrines. This seems to have been the **cult centre** of the Myceneans, where there were important buildings ornamented with wall-paintings. In one building, the 'house of the idols', archaeologists discovered numerous large clay idols, which may well have been used in religious processions.

From the west entrance of the acropolis, a paved **ramp** led up to the **palace**. It ended at a propylum with two columns of the Minoan

p. 104
Silver cup with inlaid decoration consisting of male heads in profile (thirteenth century BC, National Archaeological Museum, Athens).

type, after which came a corridor and the west entrance to the palace itself: a large stone threshold has survived. A second passage led to the central court of the palace, off which opened the three large rooms typical of all the Minoan palaces: the porch, the vestibule and the hall. In the centre of the hall are some parts of a circular hearth, surrounded by four columns. The king's throne would have stood half-way along the south wall.

The north-east side of the acropolis was occupied by a **series of workshops and storerooms**, and at the northern-most extremity of the site was the **underground cistern**. This was one of the most important examples of Mycenean architecture, because secret stores of this kind ensured the palace of a constant supply of water even when the acropolis was under siege. The cistern at Mycenae continued even out beyond the walls. It was roofed with a trough

p. 105

The Treasury of Atreus, 1250 BC, one of the most important works of Mycenaean funerary architecture.

p. 106

Above: a bronze dagger from Messinia embossed with gold molluscs (National Arch. Museum, Athens).

Below: an ivory group showing two women and a child, from Mycenae (thirteenth century BC, National Arch. Museum, Athens).

p. 107

Above: the gold mask said to be the 'Mask of Agamemnon', found at Mycenae (late sixteenth century BC, National Arch. Museum, Athens).

vault and its walls were plastered. The second **gate** to the acropolis was on the north side, and it had a courtyard and a bastion.

Outide the fortified acropolis we can see **Grave Circle B,** which dates from the seventeenth and sixteenth centuries BC. It consists of 24 shaft and cist tombs, containing bodies accompanied by rich grave offerings. Further to the south, **tombs of the Geometric period** have been discovered, along with sections of a **Hellenistic theatre** (3rd century BC) resting on the Mycenean *tholos* tomb of Clytemnestra. Many interesting finds came from the **House of Shields, the House of the Oil Merchant, the House of the Sphinxes** and the **West House**, all of which lie to the south of Grave Circle B. Among the finds were approximately 65 clay tablets with inscriptions in Linear B.

In the general area around Mycenae, many **chamber tombs** and nine *tholos* **tombs** have come to light. The *tholos* tombs are magnificent and characteristic examples of Mycenean funerary architecture. There are three categories of such tombs, and each bears a conventional name: the **tomb of the Lions, the tomb of**

Aegisthus, the tomb of Clytemnestra, the tomb of the Cylopes, the Pano Phournou tomb, the Kato Phournou tomb, the tomb of Orestes or **the Demons**, and the Treasury of Atreus. The **Treasury of Atreus** is the best-preserved prehistoric funerary monument in Europe, and the most advanced of any of the *tholos* tombs. The burial chamber is reached along the *dromos*, a corridor whose walls are faced with carefully dressed stones. The facade of the tomb is very striking, being decorated with half-columns and linear motifs in green steatite. The lintel consists of two huge slabs of stone, above which is the relieving triangle essential for the static protection of the structure. Inside, the tomb is in the shape of a beehive, with 33 courses of stone sloping gradually inwards and locked with a keystone. The interior of the *tholos* must have been decorated, as we can see from the traces of nails. Another door, also with a relieving triangle, leads into a side chamber - effectively a kind of cave, which according to some scholars functioned as an ossuary. Such instances of side chambers are rare. The name of the tomb, which dates from around 1250 BC, comes from the belief that Atreus himself had been interred in it.

p. 107

Below left: gold rings from Tiryns (fifteenth century BC) and Mycenae (sixteenth century BC, National Arch. Museum, Athens).

Below right: gold scarab from Mycenae (second half of the sixteenth century BC, National Archaeological Museum, Athens).

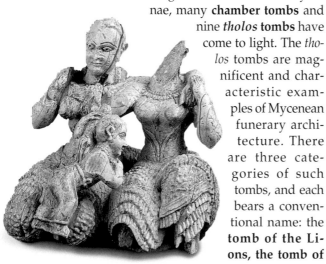

ARGOS

p. 108
Above: part of the Roman baths of Argos, mid-second century BC.

Below: view of the theatre of Argos, with a capacity of 20,000; third century BC.

According to the myths, the primo-genitor of the Argives was Inachus, whose name is borne by a river in the area. His son Phoroneus was believed by the Argives to have been the first king of the earth, and their city - which also produced a number of other important figures in the Greek myths, including Io, Danaus, Acrisius, Danae and Perseus - took its name from Argus, grandson of Phoroneus.

In Mycenean times, Argos was dependent on Tiryns and Mycenae, and it was not until after the Dorian invasion that it became one of the major Doric centres. In the seventh century BC it flourished as never before when its tyrant, Pheidon, introduced the obol, a new form of coinage, into Greece. At this time, Argos was able to extend its sovereignty over the entire Peloponnese, and was the principal rival of Sparta, with whom it was frequently at war. In the Peloponnesian War, Argos took the side of Athens, and found itself in an unenviable position when the war ended with Athenian defeat. In parallel, Argos had been developing all the forms of art. Even in Geometric times there were important pottery workshops in the city, which could also boast important sculptors in stone and bronze, such as Agelas (515-460 BC) and Policlitus (480-420 BC). Argos was the home city of Polyclitus the Younger (435-360 BC), who seems to have designed the Tholos at Epidaurus. In 229 BC, Argos joined the Achaean League, and in 146 BC it came under Roman control. In the Byzantine era, the city declined, and in 1212 it was taken by Otto de la Roche. From 1463 to 1821, with a brief interval of Venetian occupation (1686-1715), Argos was ruled by the Turks. It played an important part in the Greek War of Independence, and in 1828 was completely burned down by Ibrahim Pasha. Some fine examples of the many neo-Classical buildings which Argos once possessed have survived, including the **house of General Gordon, the municipal market** and the **barracks** which date from the time of Capodistrias.

The boundaries of the ancient city more or less coincided with those of

modern Argos, and sections of the ancient **walls** have been identified. The acropolis of Argos was located on the high hill called the **Larisa**, where two **sanctuaries,** of **Athena Polias** and **Zeus Larisaeus**, have come to light together with stretches of sixth/fifth century wall. Most of the fortifications on the acropolis were, of course, built in medieval times.

At the foot of the Larisa we can see the **theatre** of Argos, dating from the third century BC, which had a capacity of 20,000 spectators. It was used for theatrical performances, and for a while the Nemean Games were held there. It was also the venue for the assemblies of the citizens of Argos, a function for which it was to be employed again in the War of Independence, when the Fourth National Assembly of the Greeks took place there in 1829. A special structure had to be constructed in the *orchestra* of the theatre for this purpose.

To the east of the theatre are the ruins of a **baths**, standing on the site previously occupied by a first-century

p. 109
The acropolis of Larisa, to the west of the town of Argos.

sanctuary where Asclepius and the Egyptian god Sarapis were worshipped. Further south is another theatre, one of the oldest in Greece, with a capacity of 2,500 spectators. It was built in the fifth century BC and had rows of seats in straight lines and a trapezoidal *orchestra*. Here, too, the assembly of the *deme* would meet. It was replaced by a covered Odeum, which was rectangular, in the second century AD and rebuilt in a circular shape in the third century. To the south of the Odeum are traces of the **Aphrodi-sium**, a sanctuary where the cult of Aphrodite dated back to the seventh century BC.

To the east of the baths, a section of **the Agora of Argos**, destroyed by the Heruli in 267 AD, has been excavated.

The town **museum** has interesting finds from all around Argos. In the **first room** on the ground floor are Middle Helladic and Mycenean vessels and idols, Geometric pottery and bronze artefacts, Protocorinthian vases, Argive idols of the seventh and sixth centuries BC, and fragments of red-figure *craters* dating from the fifth century BC. On the **upper floor** of the Museum are finds from the excavations at the prehistoric site of Lerna. These date from between Neolithic and Mycenean times, and consist mainly of pottery and figurines. Note in particular the famous *kore*

p. 110
Head of a statue - probably the goddess Hera - from the Argive Heraeun. It is attributed to the school of painting of Polyclitus (420 BC, National Archaeological Museum, Athens).

of Lerna (a Neolithic terracotta statuette) and the large circular ceremonial hearth, dating from the Early Helladic period. On the **upper floor** are outstanding examples of Roman sculpture, most of them copies of works dating from Classical antiquity. In the **courtyard** of the Museum is a statue of Asclepius in the type known as the Guistini (a Roman copy of a fourth-century work), and there are mosaics of the second century AD from private houses in and around Argos.

The Argive Heraeum

The superb **sanctuary of Hera** stands nine kilometres from Argos. This was one of the most important Greek cult centres, and it certainly existed as far back as Mycenean times, when the Mycenean settlement of Prosymna had developed in the area. After taking and destroying Prosymna, the Argives put the sanctuary under their own protection and in the eighth century levelled the site on which the first **temple of Hera** was built a century later. This was the earliest Doric peripteral temple, and it had wooden columns, a *pronaos*, a *cella* and an *adytum*. In 423 BC the temple was destroyed by fire, but by the end of the century a new Doric temple, designed by the architect Eupolemus, had risen on a flat spot lower down to the south. Inside this temple was kept the fine chryselephantine statue of Hera by the sculptor Polyclitus. There were good sculptures on the pediments (the Birth of Zeus, the Fall of Troy) and the frieze of the temple (Battle of the Giants, Battle of the Amazons).

TIRYNS

The site at Tiryns, the third Mycenean acropolis of the Argolid and the only one to stand beside the sea (in antiquity the coastline was much closer than it is today), was excavated by Schliemann and Dörpfeld in 1884/5. The **fortifications** of Tiryns were built in sections, from south to north (lower, middle and upper acropolis) between 1375 and 1200 BC. To the north, the 'Cyclopean wall' ended in a semi-circular salient (a feature not found elsewhere in Mycenean architecture), and there are re-entrant angles on the outer side. To the west, the wall extended in a sickle-shaped sweep which was a defensive mechanism never seen before - a man-trap, as it has been called. Inside the thickness of the walls of this protrusion was a staircase which began at a postern gate to the south but

p. 111

Above: one of the storage galleries built into the thickness of the walls of the acropolis of Tiryns.

Below: wall-painting from Tiryns showing two female figures in a chariot (thirteenth century BC, National Archaeological Museum, Athens).

came
to an abrupt halt
with a gap in the floor.
In order to continue their as-
cent from here up to the acropolis, the
inhabitants would have used a kind of
drawbridge. If an attacking enemy
gained access through the postern
gate and headed up the staircase, the
drawbridge - whose existence could
not be guessed from outside - would
be removed, leaving the assailant
trapped at the gap in the floor. The
walls of Tiryns, which are unusually
thick and approximately ten metres
high,
must have impressed even
the ancients, for Homer uses the word
"*toichoessa*", 'walled', to describe the
city.

The acropolis is reached from the
east side, up a **ramp**. The defence of
the city was assisted by the maze of
narrow passages and gates in the fortifications, which ultimately lead into

during the Early Geometric period. The Mycenean *megaron* consisted of a colonnade, a vestibule and a hall. In the hall was the royal throne, and a central circular hearth surrounded by columns. The floor of the hall was ornamented with octopus and dolphin motifs set in square frames. On the walls of the *megaron* were elaborate paintings, many of which have survived and can be seen in the Archaeological Museum in Athens (the hunt of the wild goat, a procession of women, women on a chariot).

To the west of the *megaron*, archaeologists have discovered a **bath** and the drainage system of the palace. To the east was a **smaller** *megaron* of the same type as the larger palace. Beneath the two *megara* was a huge **circular structure** whose purpose is unknown to us and which was constructed around 2500 BC, in the Early Helladic period.

To the north of the *megaron* lay the **middle acropolis**, separated by a cross-wall from the **lower acropolis** further to the north. On the lower acropolis, to the north-west of the wall, were two tunnels leading to **underground cisterns** which supplied water when the palace was under siege. Excavations on the lower acropolis have revealed buildings dating from all the phases in the Bronze Age history of the palace together with sections of a **Mycenean street**.

The palace of Tiryns was destroyed in around 1200 BC, but life on the acropolis continued into the historical period. In 467 BC, the Argives dealt Tiryns its death blow at the same time as they devastated Mycenae.

two **courtyards** linked by a monumental **propylum**. From these courtyards, one could descend into the **two underground storage tunnels** of the palace, one to the east and the other to the south. These are impressive places: each consists of a corridor and a series of chambers with trough-vaulted ceilings. On the north side of the south court is a building which has been described as the **archive**, since clay tablets in Linear B script were found there, with an **off-centre propylum** leading into the **main court** of the palace. The main court had colonnades on three sides and near the entrance to it was a **circular altar** which in historical times was enclosed by a square wall. This conversion of the altar is associated with the construction of a **temple of Hera** in the *megaron*

pp. 112-113

Part of a wall-painting from Tiryns showing a wild boar hunt (thirteenth century BC, National Archaeological Museum, Athens).

NAFPLIO

Nafplio or Nauplio, chief town of the Prefecture of Argolida and one of the most attractive towns in Greece, took its name from the mythical personage Nauplius, son of Poseidon and Ammone. Nauplius' son was the sage Palamides, who gave his name to the rocky hill on which the castle stands.

The site was occupied in prehistoric times, and seems to have been an important naval power. In the seventh century BC, it came under the influence of Argos and was subsequently used as a harbour and naval base. In Roman times, the area was deserted, but fresh development took place in the Byzantine period. The Byzantines held Nauplio until 1210, when it was captured by the 'Franks'. They were followed by the Venetians (1389), the Turks (1540), Morosini at the head of the Venetian forces (1686), and the Turks again (1715). After the liberation of Greece, Nauplio was the country's first capital and the headquarters of Ioannis Capodistrias, its first governor (1829-1834). It was at Nauplio, too, that Othon, first king of Greece, landed in 1833. He was instrumental in having the capital moved to Athens.

Palamidi hill (216 m.), which can be reached up the motor road or by mounting the 857 steps on the side facing the sea, was first fortified in the second period of Venetian rule (1686-1715). Construction of the walls was begun by Morosini and completed by A. Sagredo. The castle had eight bastions, the gateways of each of which were ornamented with the Venetian coat-of-arms

p. 114

The rocky outcrop of the Acronafplia. In the background, Bourtzi.

p. 115

View of Nafplio.

The striking landscape, the historical monuments, the old houses and the narrow streets make this one of the most attractive towns in Greece.

p. 116

Above: Bourtzi, the pretty fortified island in the centre of Nafplio harbour.

Below: the rock called Palamidi towers above Nafplio and has been a powerful fortress since the second period of Venetian rule.

showing the Lion of St Mark. From the top of the historic rock, there is a panoramic view over all of Nafplio.

To the west, the city boundary is the lower hill called **Acronafplia**. Sections have survived of the fortifications built in antiquity, by the Byzantines, in Frankish times and under Venetian rule (1389-1540). Among notable features are the triangular **Grimani bastion** and a small bastion with five cannon called **'the five brothers'**.

The 'five brothers' look out across the bay to **Bourtzi**, the pretty islet off the harbour. Originally called the island of the Sts Theodore, the Bourtzi was fortified by the Venetians (1389-1540), and a boom across the harbour mouth ran from it to Acronafplia. After Liberation, the islet was the home of the executioners who dealt with those condemned to death.

The town of Nafplio is rich in historic monuments, standing here and there along the narrow cobbled streets and the fine houses of the old town. Among the most notable monuments are the **first secondary school in**

Greece and the **first teacher-pupil school**, the **Parliament building** in which the 1st National Assembly of the Greeks met in 1826, the **Army Cadet School**, the **Ministry of the Army**, the houses of **Professor Maurer** and **Count Armansperg,** regent for the young King Othon, and a **lion** carved in relief on the rock in memory of the Bavarian soldiers who died at Nafplio in an epidemic of the plague in 1833-34. Also of interest are the Venetian churches of **St Nicholas, St George** and **St Spyridon**, on the wall of which can still be seen the mark left by the bullet which killed Ioannis Capodistrias in 1831.

In Syntagma Square stands the **Archaeological Museum** of Nafplio, housed in an old Venetian barracks. On the **ground floor** are finds from the prehistoric period: Palaeolithic and Neolithic tools, Early Helladic and Mycenean pottery, a wall-painting of a priestess holding plants from the cult centre at Mycenae, large terracotta idols from the House of Idols at Mycenae and from Tiryns, a complete suit of armour found in a tomb at Dendra,

p. 117

View of Nafplio and its harbour.

together with a helmet made of the teeth of wild boars, clay tablets with Linear B script from Mycenae, funerary *stelae* from the grave precincts at Mycenae, sections of the decoration that once adorned the facade of the Treasury of Atreus, etc. The collection on display on the **upper floor** includes Geometric pottery and bronze artefacts, finds from the Argive Heraeum (statuettes, terracotta votive shields with painted decoration and terracotta masks in the form of monsters), and items from the Classical period.

pp. 118-119
The holiday village of Tolo, on the bay by the same name close to Nafplio.

LERNA

The ruins of ancient Lerna were discovered near the village of Myloi, some 10 km. from Nafplio. According to the myths, this was the place where Heracles slew the Lernaean Hydra, a monster with the body of a snake and nine heads. The excavations of J. Caskey proved that the area had been inhabited in the Neolithic period - that is, as long ago as the sixth millenium BC (Lerna I-II). The famous *kore* of Lerna, a fascinating terracotta nude female

figure, dates from the fifth or fourth millenium BC. After a period of depopulation, the site was inhabited once more in the early Bronze Age (3rd millenium BC - Lerna III), and fortified. At this time the monumental building BG was built, along with the imposing **House of Tiles**, whose remains can be seen today under their protective shelter. This was a large, two-storey building with a roof of terracotta tiles. Inside there were many rooms and long corridors, and the walls were plastered. The collection of clay seals found in one room suggest that it must have been used for administrative purposes (as an archive). The House of Tiles was destroyed before its construction was complete, in around 2000 BC, perhaps when the first Greek tribes moved into the area. At this time, a new type of arched building was introduced, and examples of these have been found on the Lerna site (Lerna IV). Lerna continued to be inhabited throughout the prehistoric period, and into Classical times (Lerna V-VII). The finds from Lerna are on display in the museum of Argos.

p. 119
Above: View of the town of Nafplio.

Below: the Bavarian Lion, a monument carved out of the rock to commemorate the Bavarian soldiers who died in an epidemic in Greece in 1833-1834.

pp. 120-121

The famous theatre at Epidaurus, fourth century BC.

Below: Corinthian column from the colonnade inside the Tholos at Epidaurus (Epidaurus Museum).

EPIDAURUS

Epidaurus, as the best-known sanctuary of the healer-god Asclepius, was one of the most important religious sites of the ancient world. According to the myths, Asclepius was the son of Apollo and Coronis, and he learned the art of medicine from his father and from Cheiron, the wise Centaur. Apollo was initially worshipped at Epidaurus with the epithet 'Maleatas', a reflection of the cult of a pre-Dorian deity whose sanctuary predated that of Apollo on the slopes of Mt Cynortium. At the time of the Dorian invasion, the two gods became identified and were worshipped on the same site. After the mid-sixth century BC, the sanctuary was extended to the south, and occupied the flat site where the Asclepium was later built. At the end of the same century, the cult of Asclepius was introduced from Thessaly, and gradually displaced that of Apollo. Not, of course, that the **sanctuary of Apollo Maleatas** on Mt Cynortium ever ceased to function: the ruins of a fourth-century temple of Apollo and of other buildings have been excavated there.

Over time, the renown of Asclepius spread throughout the known world and the flow of patients to his sanctuary swelled. At this time, too, the foundations of the science of medicine were being laid, and diagnosis came to be based more on observation of the patient's symptoms than on the earlier 'metaphysical' approach. After sacrifice and purification, the patients would enter the sanctuary and would sleep in a special place - the *abaton*

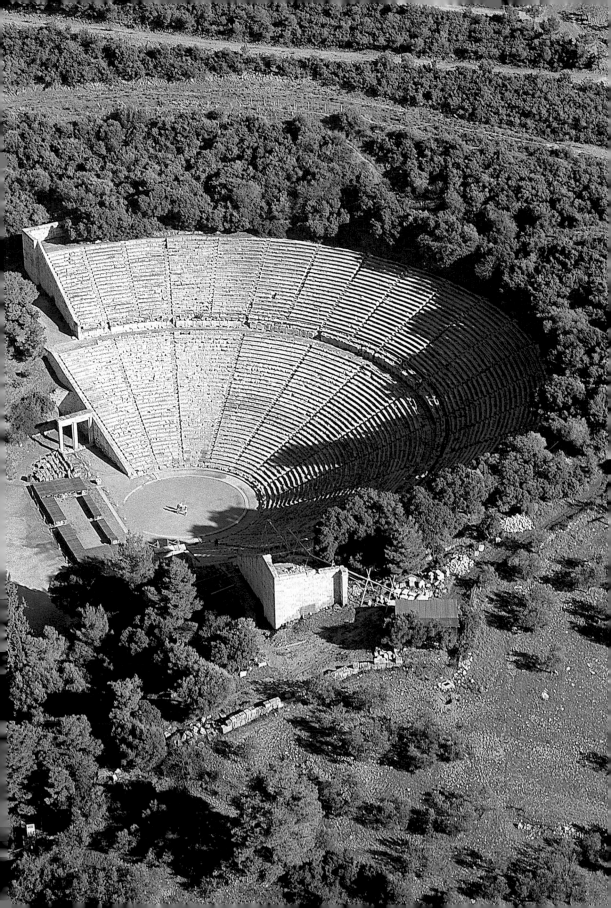

or *encoemeterium* - in which the god would reveal to them, in dream, how they could be cured, or even effect the cure himself at that time.

The **Asclepium** of Epidaurus reached the peak of its fame in the late fifth and early fourth century. Important buildings were constructed at that time, and precious statues and pillars with inscriptions were dedicated to the healer-god. In 86 BC, the sanctuary was looted by Sulla, but in the second century AD new buildings were erected and others repaired with funds donated by a Roman senator called Antoninus. The Emperor Theodosius suppressed the cult of Asclepius in the fourth century AD, and severe earthquakes

*pp. 122-123
Views of the theatre at Epidaurus, where perhaps the world's finest performances of the ancient drama take place every summer.*

in 522 and 551 laid waste the site.

In antiquity, access to the sanctuary was from the north, but today the entrance to the archaeological site is on the south side. The most important buildings revealed by archaeological excavation are as follows:

- The **Catagogium:** this was a kind of hotel, dating from the fourth/third century BC and consisting of four square blocks, each with two storeys of rooms round a square, colonnaded court. - The **odeum and temple of Hygeia**: built in the Roman period on the site of a Gymnasium or refectory of 300 BC. - The **Stadium**: built in the early fifth century, with stone seating dating from the fourth century BC. To the south of the stadium must have

been the **Hippodrome** (late 5th century), and to the north of it was the **Palaestra**, while a building to the east which used to be taken for the Palaestra has now been identified as the **shrine** of a mystic cult. - The **temple of Artemis**: dating from around 300 BC, this was a Doric prostyle structure with a Π-shaped interior colonnade of Corinthian columns. To the east was an altar, reached from the temple along a paved path. - **Building E**: an early *encoemeterium*, of the second half of the fifth century BC, this stood on a site previously occupied by an altar of ash and a small temple of Apollo. - The **Tholos** (Rotunda): this circular structure was built in 360-320 by Polyclitus the Younger. The columns on the outside were in the Doric order, and those inside were Corinthian. The *metopes* were ornamented only with rosettes. The coffered ceiling panels, on the other hand, were richly ornamented. The wealth of ornamental detail of the Tholos marks the beginning of the end of Classical austerity. From a crypt in the *cella* it was possible to descend into an underground space laid out as a labyrinth, which may well have been used for a subterranean cult of Asclepius. The use of this striking building has never been satisfactorily explained. - **The temple of Asclepius** (380-375 BC): a Doric peripteral structure without an *opisthodomos* and with a Π-shaped interior colonnade of Ionic or Corinthian

two Doric colonnades, one to the north and one to the south, with an interior Corinthian colonnade.

On the slopes of Mt Cynortium is the **theatre** of Epidaurus, the best-preserved ancient theatre in Greece. Its construction was bound up with the process of therapy, and was thus not unconnected with the cult of Asclepius: it was believed that theatrical performances, by entertaining the visitors to the sanctuary, speeded up their cure. Pausanias tells us that the theatre was designed by the architect Polyclitus the Younger, but archaeological research has questioned this, giving the theatre a later date somewhere around the end of the fourth or the beginning of the third century BC. Originally, the theatre had a circular *orchestra* with the *thymele* in the centre and twelve wedges of 34 rows of seats, giving a total capacity of about 6,000. In the second century BC, the upper tier, with a further 22 rows of seats, was added, thus providing seating for an audience of 12,300. The first row of seats in both the upper and the lower tiers were for officials and took the form of thrones. The acting area was entered through *parodoi* at the sides, where there were Ionic gateways. The *skene* itself had two storeys, consisting of a *proscenium*, a raised *logeum* and two *parascenia*. The harmonious proportions of the Epidaurus theatre and the beauty of the surrounding landscape combined with the exceptional acoustics of the theatre to create a unique impression. The acoustics are the result of the fact that the *orchestra* is slightly elliptical and not a perfect circle, with three distinct sound lines. Today, the atmosphere of the theatre

columns. This was the first temple in which the symmetry of Classical times began to give way to accentuation of the facade. Its architect was called Theodotus, while the chryselephantine cult statue of Asclepius was the work of the Parian sculptor Thrasymedes. The sculpted ornamental work was the work of the renowned artist Timotheus. On the east pediment was the Fall of Troy, and on the west the Battle of the Amazons. Victories and personified Breezes on horseback were used as *acroteria* (National Archaeological Museum, Athens). To the east was an elongated **altar** for sacrifices. - The **Abaton** (*encoemeterium*): the place in which patients were treated by the method known as incubation was an unusual stoa consisting of two sections. The east part (4th century BC) had Ionic columns, and in it was the sacred spring for purification, where there were inscriptions relating to cures. The west section had two storeys, and was built in the Hellenistic or Roman period at a slightly lower level. - The **temple of Themis**: of the fourth century BC. - The **Propylaea**:

p. 124
View of the archaeological site of the Asklepiun at Epidaurus.

can be enjoyed during one of the performances of the ancient drama held every summer as part of the Epidaurus Festival.

At the entrance to the archaeological site is a **museum** with the finds from the Asclepium. In the **first room** are inscriptions with medical prescriptions and details of cures, statues of the Hellenistic period, medical instruments, lamps and terracotta offerings to the god. The **second room** contains a collection of votive statues, plaster casts of statues from the Asclepium (the originals are in the National Archaeological Museum in Athens), and architectural members from the Temple of Artemis. In the **third room** is a reconstruction of the Doric entablature of the temple of Asclepius, together with sections of the Tholos and a superb Corinthian column capital used as a model for the columns in the Tholos.

At a distance of 18 km. from the Asclepium is the village of **Palaia Epidavros,** where excavation work has been done on the **settlement of ancient Epidaurus** and a stone **theatre** of the late fourth century BC. Theatrical performances are held there, too. At Nea Epidavros are the ruins of a medieval **castle**, while a little further to the north is **Agnoundos Monastery,** with Byzantine wall-paintings.

p. 125

The foundations of the Tholos at Epidaurus, as they are today (fourth century BC).

PATRA - RIO

Patra is the chief town of the Prefecture of Achaia and one of the most important harbours for communications between Greece and Western Europe. The site was occupied in Mycenean times, and it can be assumed that the Achaeans moved in after the Mycenean centres had been destroyed. Between this time and the end of the Classical period, the settlement was of an agricultural nature and took little part in the shared activities of the Greeks. Under the Romans, however, it flourished, and became a centre for commerce and industry. St Andrew, patron saint of Patra, taught the Gospel in the city and was martyred there in 68 AD. Justinian walled Patra in the late sixth century AD, and after the seventh century the local people acquired considerable revenue from the production of silk. In the thirteenth century, Patra was the feudal estate of Guillaume Aleman of Provence, and the seat of a Latin archbishop. Over the centuries which followed, possession of Patra alternated between Venetians and Turks (Venetian occupation: 1408-1430 and 1687-1715), and in 1828 the city was liberated by General Maison. Today, the city is divided into Upper and Lower parts, and is notable for its good planning, its wide streets, its plentiful gardens and its spacious squares.

Of the ancient city, only the Roman Odeum has survived, in the area which must have been occupied by the ancient Agora. The **Odeum** of Patra was constructed in the second century AD. The traveller Pausanias believed it to be inferior only to the Herodes Atticus Theatre in Athens, commenting in particular on its interior marble facings and the rich ornamentation of mosaics on the floor of the *skene*.

Above the bustling harbour of Patra is the **castle hill**, where parts of the Byzantine fortifications and the subsequent repairs to them have survived.

Patra has an **Archaeological Museum** with a collection including Roman sculptures, pottery and miniature artefacts dating from between Mycenean times and the Roman period, mosaics, weapons, etc.

p. 126
Above: view of the city of Patra today.
Below: the church of St Andrew, patron saint of Patra.

Approximately 10 km. to the east of Patra is **Rio**, from which ferries ply across to **Antirrio** on the shore of Central Greece. In antiquity, the two facing headlands were called Rion of Achaea and Rion of Aetolia. The fortresses that stand on them were originally built in 1499 by the Sultan Bayazid II. Almost nothing of this phase of building has survived, since the castles were wrecked by the Knights of Malta in 1603. The forts we see at Rio and Antirrio today were constructed by the Venetians in 1701-1713.

that in 1463 Ekaterini Palaeologina threw herself from the walls of the **castle of Oria**, just outside Kalavryta, rather than be taken alive by the Turks. Seven kilometres from Kalavryta is the **Monastery of Ayia Lavra**, founded in 961 by Athanasius of Athos 300 metres to the east of its current site, to which it moved in 1689. In 1821, the banner of the Greek War of Independence was raised here and the freedom fighters were sworn in. In 1943, the monastery was burned by the Germans.

p. 127

Above: Kalavryta, the terminus of the mountain railway which leads up, through superb scenery, from Diakofto.

Below: the Monastery of Ayia Lavra, near Kalavryta.

DIAKOFTO - MEGA SPILAIO - KALAVRYTA

Diakofto is an attractive resort village on the coast of the Gulf of Corinth. It is also the starting-point for the rack-and-pinion railway which climbs up through the Vouraikos gorge, in a landscape of unparalleled grandeur. Near the verdant village of **Zachlorou** is the **Monastery of Mega Spilaio**, at an altitude of 924 m. In the fourth century, a small section of what was later to become a large foundation was built by the monks Theodore and Symeon in the side of a steep cliff on Mt Chelmos. Over the centuries, more and more buildings were added, but the monastery was burned by the Germans in 1943 and reconstructed in the form we see today. In a cavern dedicated to Our Lady of the Golden Cave is a miraculous icon of the Virgin which is locally believed to have been painted by St Luke.

The end of the railway line is at **Kalavryta**, among the foothills of the Aroania Mountains. There is an old story

OLYMPIA

p. 128
Above: the temple of Hera at Olympia, 600 BC.
Below: the head of the statue of Apollo which ornamented the central section of the west pediment of the temple of Zeus (470-456 BC).

O lympia was the most sacred of the sanctuaries of the ancient Greeks. It was the place in which Zeus, chief among the gods, was worshipped, and where the Olympic Games were held in his honour. The significance of the Games is manifest in the number of Greek city-states that participated in them, honouring the truce traditionally imposed during each Olympic period, and in the fact that the Olympiad - that is, the period of four years from one Games to the next - was recognised as the sole reliable system of chronology throughout Greece.

History

The sanctuary and its surroundings were first inhabited in the Early Helladic period (third millenium BC). In the **sanctuary of Zeus**, archaeologists have discovered **six arched buildings** of 2200-2000 BC, together with a tomb around which a cult centred, called the **Pelopeum** (2500 BC). The Pelopeum is connected with Pelops, who according to the myths was victorious in a chariot race over Oenomaus, king of Pisa. Sure enough, the sanctuary was originally controlled by Pisa, later passing into the hands of Elis, which was responsible for organising the Olympic Games. Before the Dorian invasion, Olympia would seem to have been a centre for cults connected with the earth. On the **hill of Cronium**, to the north of the archaeological site, the cult of Cronus devel-

◄ *p. 129*
Part of the Palaestra in the sanctuary of Zeus at Olympia.

p. 130
Above: Part of the Palaestra.
Below: columns from sacred buildings in the archaeological site of Olympia.

oped, and on the south-west slope of the hill there must have been a **shrine of Gaea**. When the Dorians invaded, the old chthonic deities were replaced by the new sky-gods, Zeus and Hera. On the other hand, the Mycenean king Pelops continued to be honoured, and in his cult would seem to lie the roots of the games which were later established in honour of Zeus. The first Olympic Games were held by Iphitus, King of Elis, in 776 BC. After the fifth century BC, the Games became renowned throughout the Greek world, and the sanctuary of Zeus acquired priceless votive offerings and superb buildings. In 74 BC, Olympia was looted by Sulla, and in 67 AD Nero carried off much of the statuary from the site to Rome - after first competing in the Games and winning six events. In 393 AD, the Emperor Theodosius II ordered the destruction of the temples, a task in which he was assisted by a series of severe earthquakes. The excavations on the site have been largely the work of the German Archaeological Institute, beginning in 1875.

The sanctuary of Zeus

The sanctuary of Zeus was marked out on the north side by Cronium hill and on the west and south sides by the rivers Cladeus and Alpheius, respectively. Inside the sanctuary, a wall dating as far back as the Geometric period showed the boundaries of the **Altis** (or grove), the densely-vegetated precinct of Zeus. We enter the archaeological site from an entrance on the north, and can see the following buildings:
- The **Prytaneum** of the Elians: this was constructed in the sixth century BC and repaired on quite a number of occasions down to Roman times. Inside the Prytaneum the sacred flame of the Elians was kept. - The **Philippeum**: this was a circular building or *tholos* in the Ionic order, built in 338 BC by Philip II of Macedon and his son Alexander. It housed chryselephantine statues of Philip and his family, the work of the famous sculptor Leochares. The **Heraeum**: the temple of Hera, where Zeus was also worshipped until 460 BC, was built in 600 BC. It was a Doric peripteral temple with a *pronaos* and an *opis-*

p. 131
The palaestra, to the west of the Altis, was where the athletes trained for the contests in wrestling, boxing and jumping; third century BC.

p. 132

Above: the arched entrance leading to the Stadium at Olympia.
Below: the Stadium at Olympia, where the Olympic Games of antiquity were held.

thodomos, both distyle *in antis*. The columns of the *cella* were originally wood and over the years were replaced by wooden columns, one by one: Pausanias, in the second century AD, saw the last wooden column still in place. In his day, the temple was used as a kind of exhibition hall for statues, among which was the famous Hermes of Praxiteles. - The **Nymphaeum**: this dedication to the Nymphs was constructed by Herodes Atticus and his wife Regilla in 149-153 AD. It was a sumptuous structure with statues of the imperial family

of the Antonines, of the founders and of Zeus. - The **altar of Heracles**: Heracles, the Doric hero *par excellence*, was viewed as the founder of the Olympic Games because he was traditionally supposed to have sacrificed a black ram at the cenotaph of Pelops. - The **Treasuries**: these were built slightly above the level of the site, on the side of Cronium hill, and most of them date from the sixth or fifth century BC. Their arrangement in a straight line reflects the spirit of equality and unity that linked the city-states of Greece at the time of the Olympic Games. Five of the 12 treasuries have been identified with certainty; they belonged to **Sikyon, Selinus, Metapontum, Megara** and **Gela**. Most of the treasuries were built by Doric cities - given that Olympia was the centre of the Dorian tribe - and especially by those in the West. In among the treasuries was an Archaic **altar of Gaea**. - The **Zannes**: in front of the treasuries stand the plinths of sixteen bronze statues to Zeus, the money for which was contributed compulsorily, as a kind of fine, by those who were discovered to have won at Olympia by cheating. - The **Metroön**: this Doric peripteral temple to Rhea-Cybele, mother of the gods, was built in 400-390 BC. In the time of Augustus, it was used for the Emperor's own cult. The Metroön was destroyed in 267 AD. - The **Stadium**: the Stadium was moved to its present position, outside the boundaries of the Altis, at some point in the fifth or fourth century BC, when the Games had lost their religious significance and had become a purely secular event. The Olympic Games lasted five days and included contests for buglers and heralds as well as the boys' events, horse races and the athletic contests: the

pentathlon, the foot race, wrestling, boxing, the *pancratium* and the race for warriors in armour. The winners of the various events received a *cotinus* or wreath of wild olive, cut from the tree which was believed to have been planted by Heracles. The stadium had a length of 600 Greek feet: 192 metres. The spectators sat on the ground all around the stadium, though there were stone thrones for the official representatives of the city-states, the organisers of the Games, the *Hellanodices* or umpires, and the priestess of Demeter Chamyne, the only woman allowed to watch the events. The Stadium was entered along a vaulted passage built on the west side in the third century BC. - The **Echo Colonnade**: this was built in the second half of the fourth century BC in order to separate the Altis from the Stadium. On its facade, it had Corinthian columns, with Doric columns inside, and there was a line of rooms. In front of the colonnade were numerous votive statues. - The **statues and votive offerings** to Zeus, which clustered around the temple of the god, were often works of outstanding artistry. Among the pedestals of these statues is that of the famous Nike by the sculptor Paeonius, set up by the exiled Messenians of Naupactus after their victory over the Spartans at Sphacteria in 425 BC. - The **Temple of Zeus** (470-456 BC): this temple, built in shell-limestone and marble, represents the ultimate achievement of the Doric order. It was peripteral, with *pronaos* and an *opisthodomos*, both distyle *in antis*, and its *cella* was divided into three aisles by two-tiered colonnades which supported galleries. The temple stood on a platform and was of huge dimensions (length 60 m., width 23 m., height approximately 20 m.). Its

architect was Libon of Argos, while the chryselephantine statue of Zeus in the temple, one of the seven wonders of the world, was by Phidias. The god, 12.5 metres high, was seated - and gave visitors the impression that if he were to stand up he would lift the roof off the temple. He held a Victory in one hand and in the other a sceptre with the eagle, his symbol, and he was decorated with jewellery consisting of precious stones. On the pedestal were reliefs, and the floor - of grey limestone from Eleusis - contained a depression filled

p. 133

The fifth-century basilica on the site previously occupied by the workshop of Phidias.

with oil which was used for the maintenance of the statue and which also, because of the reflections in it, enhanced the visual impression made by the statue. On the pediments of the temple were sculptures depicting the preparations for the chariot-race between Pelops and Oenomaus (east side) and the Battle of the Centaurs (west side), while the friezes of the *pronaos* and *opisthodomos* showed the Twelve Labours of Heracles. The temple of Zeus was shattered by an earthquake in the sixth century AD. - The **workshop of Phidias**: the cult statue of Zeus was made in the workshop of the great sculptor, which stood to the west of the temple. Materials and tools for the carving of stone and the making of gold artefacts have been found in the workshop, along with a small terracotta *oenochoe* marked with the inscription "I BELONG TO PHIDIAS". The findings in the building allow it to be dated to 438-430 BC. In the fifth century AD, an Early Christian basilica was erected on the same site, and its ruins can be seen today. - the **Theocoleum**: this building, of the Classical period, was the official residence of the priests at Olympia. - The **Heroön**: this building contained an antechamber and two rooms, one of which was circular and must have been the premises of some early cult. It seems to have been used as a bath before the first century BC. - The **Roman hostel and baths**: three such groups of

p. 134
A small earthenware wine-cup with the inscription "I belong to Phidias" on its base (Olympia Museum).

buildings have come to light, on the west, south and east sides of the site. - The **Leonidium**: this was the public hostel of Olymia, built around 330 BC with funds donated by Leonidas of Naxos. The Leonidium was the largest structure in the sanctuary, and it had rooms arranged round a courtyard with a Doric colonnade. Outside, an Ionic colonnade ran right round the building, giving it the appearance of a temple and offsetting the *hubris* that the construction of such an enormous building might have been thought to imply. In the time of Hadrian, the Leonidium was used as a residence for Roman officials, and its central courtyard was redesigned as a garden with winding channels of water, a central 'island', and bridges to allow the residents to move about. This layout was a replica in miniature of Hadrian's villa at Tivoli. - The **South Stoa** (Praesidium): this was built in the fourth century BC and formed the south boundary of the precinct. It had Doric columns on the outside and Corinthian columns within. On the facade was a platform from which the officials may have watched the horsemen and chariots as they headed for the Hippodrome to race. The **Hippodrome** itself must have been somewhere further south, in line with the Stadium. - The **Bouleuterium**: this consisted of two buildings with apses dating from the sixth century BC, between which was a rectangular structure added, with the Doric porch on the east, in the fourth century BC. The Bouleuterium contained the **altar of Zeus Horceus**, at which the athletes took the oath to honour the rules of the Games. - The **Palaestra** (3rd century BC): the ruins of the Palaestra can be seen by the north entrance. Here the athletes practised for the 'heavy' events (wrestling, boxing, the *pancratium*). There were rooms arranged around a central court with a Doric colonnade. The rooms themselves, which were baths, stores for the olive oil used by the athletes, dressing-rooms, and areas for training in bad weather or for philo- sophical discussion, had Ionic columns on the side facing the court. - The **Gymnasium**: the gymnasium was located to the north of the palaestra, and could be reached from it through a gate. It consisted of four Doric and Ionic colonnades and was used for training in the 'light' events (2nd century BC).

OLYMPIA MUSEUM

Close to the archaeological site is **Olympia Museum**, whose contents include finds of inestimable value. In the **vestibule** is an excellent model of the site. **Room I**: prehistoric finds from the area around Olympia, and bronze exhibits of the Geometric period. **Room II**: exhibits from the Archaic period: bronze and terracotta figurines of humans and animals, bronze plates with scenes in relief, an important collection of weapons dedicated as offerings to the sanctuary of Zeus, a colossal limestone head of a goddess (600 BC) which probably came from the temple of Hera, and the terracotta *acroterium* from the top of the temple of Hera. **Room III**: exhibits of the Archaic period: terracotta and bronze vessels and figurines, a section of the painted terracotta facing of the pediment from the treasury

p. 135

Sections of the sculptures showing the Battle of the Centaurs from the west pediment of the temple of Zeus (Olympia Museum - temple of Zeus sculpture room)

p. 136

Above: part of the pediment showing the Battle of the Centaurs from the temple of Zeus (Olympia Museum).

of Gela, and a reconstruction of a section of the entablature from the treasury of Megara; **Room IV** (the Classical period): a terracotta group of 480-470 BC showing Zeus carrying off Ganymede, bronze votive offerings of the 'severe order' period, a terracotta head of Athena dating from 490 BC, the finds from the workshop of Phidias, the helmet worn by Miltiades at Marathon, and Roman statuary. **Room V**: this is the most important room in the entire museum, containing as it does the sculptures from the temple of Zeus, works of the highest artistic value in the severe style of the early fifth century BC. On display are the 12 *metopes* from the short sides of the temple, which with unique symmetry and power depict the Labours of Heracles, the lion's head water-spouts from the roof, and - most important of all - the pedimental sculptures, among the most sublime creations of antiquity. The pediments, almost completely in Par-

ian marble (some of the figures are in marble from Mt Pendeli), have been reconstructed in accordance with their surviving sections. On the east pediment we see the myth of the chariot race between Pelops and Oenomaus, with Zeus as the central figure, and on the west is the Battle of the Centaurs, taking place around the figure of Apollo. **Room VI**: finds from the Late Classical and Hellenistic phase in the sanctuary's history. **The Hermes Room**: here we see the marble statue of Hermes (340-330 BC), found in the temple of Hera, a work of incomparable artistry which is attributed to the famous sculptor Praxiteles. **The Roman Room**: statues of the Roman period. **The Olympic Games Room**: finds from the sanctuary which are connected with the Games and with athletic activities in general (pieces of sporting equipment, offerings dedicated by victors).

p. 136

Below: head of a terracotta statue of Athena found at Olympia (490 BC, Olympia Museum).

p. 137

The Hermes of Praxiteles (Olympia Museum).

TEGEA

Ancient Tegea was among the most important cities of Arcadia, and it was formed by the amalgamation of a number of smaller cities. Today, at the archaeological site we can see sections of the ancient **wall**, the **agora**, a **theatre** of the second century BC, a **sanctuary of Demeter** and the famous shrine of **Athena Alea**. This was a cult centre as far back as Mycenean times, while the first stone temple, with apses, in honour of **Alea**, a fertility and war goddess, was built in the Geometric period. Alea soon became identified with Athena, and around 600 BC the cult moved to a new temple with wooden columns and an entablature, inside which was a small ivory cult statue by the sculptor Endoeus. The statue was unharmed when the temple burned down in 395 BC. Building of a stone Doric temple to Athena Alea, designed and ornamented by the famous sculptor Scopas of Paros, was complete by 335 BC. The sculptures which ornamented the temple showed scenes from the Labours of Heracles, from the myth of the local hero Telephus, and from the hunting of the Calydonian Boar. A tradition tells us that the teeth of the Caly-

p. 138
The head of a marble statue of the goddess Hygeia, from the sanctuary of Athena Alea at Tegea, by the famous sculptor Scopas (360 BC, National Archaeological Museum, Athens).

donian Boar had been entrusted to the temple and were kept there. To the east was the **altar** of Athena Alea, of the Ionic type, which bore a relief showing scenes from the birth of Zeus among Nymphs and the Nine Muses (4th century BC). In the modern village of Tegea is a **museum** in which one can admire what has survived of the wonderful sculptures of Scopas and of the architectural members of the buildings in the area.

BASSAE (VASSES), PHIGALEIA

In the mountainous area near Phigaleia, Apollo was worshipped in antiquity with the epithet 'Epicurius'. A temple to him was first dedicated in the seventh century BC, and this was rebuilt twice (in 600 BC and 500 BC) before the construction, late in the fifth century BC, of the last and most important temple, the work of the great architect Ictinus. The temple, which has been partially reconstructed and is surrounded by a protective tent, was discovered in 1765 by the French architect J. Bocher, and subsequently attracted the attention of many travellers. In 1812, a group of 'antiquarians' consisting of artists and literary figures removed many of the architectural members, which later found their way to the British Museum.

The temple of Apollo was constructed in accordance with a pioneering architectural design in which the

influence of the Parthenon can be detected. This was a peripteral structure
with elements from the Doric order
(the outer columns) as well as from
the Ionic and Corinthian. All around
the interior of the *cella* was an Ionic
frieze with sculptures showing the
Battle of the Amazons and the Battle
of the Centaurs, and this was the first
time the interior of a temple had been
decorated. The artist's desire to draw
attention to the interior is also evident
in the way the Ionic colonnades of the
cella were engaged in the walls so as to
leave plenty of free space. The two
colonnades enclosed, on the south
side, a single Corinthian column. The
capital of this column has disap-
peared, but drawings of it have survived and thus we know it was the
earliest Corinthian capital yet dis-

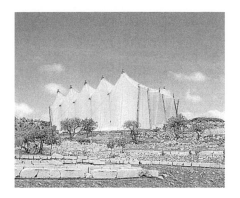

covered. Behind the *cella* was an *adyton*
in which sacred rituals were conduct-
ed and where the statue of the god was
kept. The temple of Apollo Epicurus at
Bassae is one of the most important
monuments of antiquity, one which,
thanks to the genius of Ictinus, represented a new departure in the evolu-
tion of ancient Greek architecture.

p. 139

*The temple of
Apollo at Bassae
near Phigaleia.
Above: the temple
is enveloped in
canvas to protect
it from the
elements.*

SPARTA (SPARTI)

p. 140

Above: view of Sparta.

Below: statue of a running hoplite, possibly Leonidas (early fifth century, Sparta Museum).

Modern Sparti, standing on the same site as its ancient counterpart, is the chief town of the Prefecture of Lakonia. Although ancient Sparta was among the most important ancient Greek city-states, little has survived of its buildings, largely as a result of the austerity for which the Spartans were renowned. The military orientation of their life-style left little scope for the erection of sumptuous monuments, a point of which the ancient historian Thucydides was fully aware: "If Lacedaemon is ever destroyed", he wrote, "and only its shrines and the foundations of its public buildings survive, then those who come there in the future will find it hard to believe that the power of the city was equal to its reputation".

We can see from the Homeric epics that in the Mycenean period Sparta was one of the strongest cities in Greece. Helen, who according to the myth was the cause of the Trojan War, was the wife of Menelaus, king of Sparta and brother of Agamemnon. However, very few traces dating back to Mycenean times have come to light in Sparta, and our knowledge of the city's importance is based largely on literary sources. Around 1100 BC, the Dorians reached the Peloponnese and settled in the towns of Pitane, Limnae, Mesoa and Cynosura in the valley of the river Eurotas. Sparta was thus, in effect, a *synoecismus*, and it retained this form of organisation even when the city-state was the predominant unit throughout the rest of Greece. The Dorians of Sparta

ΜΟΛΩΝ ΛΑΒΕ

ΤΟΝΔΕ ΑΝΔΡΙΑΝΤΑ
ΒΑΣΙΛΕΩΣ ΛΕΩΝΙΔΑ
ΣΥΝ ΤΩ ΗΡΩΩ ΤΟΥΤΩ
Ο ΕΚ ΛΑΚΕΔΑΙΜΟΝΟΣ
ΠΑΝΟΣ Σ. ΚΟΥΜΑΝΤΑΡΟΣ
ΤΗ ΣΠΑΡΤΗ ΑΝΕΘΗΚΕΝ
1968

subdued Laconia and overcame the Messenians in a series of wars called the Messenian Wars. When Dorian dominion was complete, the pre-Dorian populations and the people of the conquered surrounding areas made up the classes, respectively, of the *helots* and the *perioeci*.

In the Classical period, the Spartans differed from the rest of Greece both in the system by which they governed themselves and in their way of life. The Spartan system of government is usually described as oligarchic, but it did have some democratic features. The city was administered by the kings, the senate, the ephors and the *apella*. The kings, of whom there were two - one each from the Agid and Eury-pontid families - shared power, and were thus able to exercise control over each other. The senate consisted of the two kings and 28 men over 60 years of age, who held their posts for life. The senate's role was to prepare the agenda of subjects to be discussed at the assembly of the people, and although its role was consultative it was very influential in Spartan affairs. Each of the five 'towns' of Sparta (Amyclae had been added in the eighth century BC) was represented by an Ephor, and the Ephors were responsible to the people for controlling the kings

and serving as a court of justice in the event of offences. The citizens themselves were represented by the *apella, whose members consisted of male Spartans over the age of 30.* The *apella* elected the members of the senate and the ephors, and it decided - by acclaim - on matters of war or peace. Lycurgus, who is considered to have flourished in the eighth century BC, was traditionally believed to have established the Spartan system of government and the laws of the city.

Sparta was a military society *par excellence*, which was largely the result of the fact that the city had to control a

◄ *p. 141*

A modern statue of Leonidas erected in the town of Sparta.

p. 142

Part of a mosaic floor from the vicinity of Sparta , showing the Athenian statesman Alcibiades (second or third century AD, Sparta Museum).

large number of unenfranchised citizens and subservient peoples who could be expected to rise in revolt at any time. The lives of the Spartans were dedicated to the service of the city and to the arts of war. At the age of seven, the boys were already being trained in strict discipline, and between eighteen and thirty they served in the Spartan army, often living far from their homes and wives and being subjected to a harsh military regime. The women, too, underwent physical training, and enjoyed more freedom than their counterparts elsewhere in Greece.

It was in these conditions that Sparta developed into one of the leading Greek powers in the late sixth century BC. It played a major part in resistance to the Persians in the early fifth century, but its disputes with Athens, its great rival, ultimately led to the Peloponnesian War. Despite victory in the war, Sparta began to decline, and in 371 BC was defeated by Thebes at the battle of Leuctra. In the third century BC, it put up stout resistance to the Macedonians, but was unable to avoid subservience to them. In 192 BC, it acceded to the Achaean League, and in 146 BC was conquered by Rome,

p. 143

The centre of the town of Sparta, with Mt Taygetos in the background.

which granted a certain degree of au-to-nomy to the coastal regions around Sparta. These areas became known as the *koinon* of the Free Laconians. In the second and third centuries AD, Sparta enjoyed a late flowering, but before long it was devastated by raids from Alaric and the Slavs and the popula-tion fled to the Mani. The Byzantines repopulated the city, calling it Lacedaemonia. After the battle of Pelagonia in 1262, these new inhabi-tants moved to Mystras. The construc-tion of the modern city of Sparta be-gan in the time of King Othon.

Ancient Sparta had no walls until the third century BC, when a circular **precinct** was constructed around the

p. 144
Laconian relief showing Castor and Pollux, the Heavenly Twins (sixth century AD, Sparta Museum).

four 'towns'. On the **acropolis** of Spar-ta was a most important temple, dedi-cated to **Athena Chalcioecus or Poli-uchus**, which was built on the site of a shrine dating back to the time of Ly-curgus and serving as an inviolable sanctuary. The epithet 'chalcioecus', meaning 'of the bronze house', may come from the fact that the interior of the temple was lined with metal plaques bearing scenes in relief and that the cult statue, by the sculptor Gi-tiadas, was also bronze. The acropolis of Sparta has also yielded the ruins of a **theatre** built during the Hellenistic period and reconstructed by the Ro-mans. To the north-east of the theatre are traces of a **tenth-century basilica** dedicated to the Blessed Nicon, a local Spartan saint.

The **sanctuary of Artemis Orthia** has been excavated to the east of the acropolis, by the main road from Tripoli to Sparta. The first **temple** to the goddess was built around 700 BC, and was replaced by a Doric structure in 570 BC. Early in the third century BC an **amphitheatre** was constructed in the precinct, but the temple was left standing in the centre of the *skene*. At the **altar** to the east of the temple were held the flogging ceremonies which, in ancient times, were connected with the transition from adolescence to man-hood. The flogging, with the branches of trees, was also a symbol of the infu-sion in the youths of the powers of life, since Orthia, the deity originally wor-shipped in the sanctuary and later con-flated with Artemis, was a fertility goddess. In rituals of a different kind held in honour of the goddess, the par-ticipants wore ceremonial masks in the shape of monsters, some of which have been found in the sanctuary.

To the north of the modern town are the ruins of what is often called the **tomb of Leonidas**. According to the tradition, this is the spot at which Leonidas of Sparta, who fell to preserve his city's honour in the battle of Thermopylae, was buried.

Five kilometres to the south-east of Sparta, archaeologists have discovered a sanctuary dedicated to Menelaus and Helen (the **Menelaeum**). The ruins of the sanctuary - on top of Profitis Ilias hill - date from the fifth century BC, although a cult had developed in the area as far back as Mycenean times.

Six kilometres to the south of Sparta is the city of **Amyclae**, on whose acropolis Apollo was worshipped. In his **sanctuary**, on the hill of Ayia Kyriaki, the **tomb and altar of Hyacinthus**, a pre-Dorian local hero, was located. When the area was annexed by Sparta, Hyacinthus and Apollo became identified. A colossal statue of Apollo, 13 metres high, surrounded by colonnades, was erected on the tomb of Hyacinthus. The site was laid out by Bathycles of Magnesia in Asia Minor some time around the mid-sixth century BC.

At **Vapheio**, close to Amyclae, a Mycenean tholos tomb containing a large hoard of gold funerary offerings was discovered. Among the finds were the two superb gold cups with hunting scenes in relief now to be seen in the Archaeological Museum in Athens.

Sparta has an **archaeological museum** built in 1876-78 to plans by the Danish architect Hansen. The prehistoric collection contains some outstanding examples of Mycenean pottery, and there are fine Geometric and Archaic vases. Among the notable pottery and bronze exhibits are the terracotta ritual monster masks from the sanctuary of Artemis Orthia and the *stelae* with sickles dedicated to the goddess by the youths who were victorious in the contests in her honour. Of particular interest is the torso of a warrior dating from around 480 BC and believed to be a depiction of Leonidas. The reliefs of Castor and Pollux (the Dioscuri), who were worshipped as chthonic deities and were often depicted with their sister Helen and with Menelaus, are typical of Spartan art.

Among the remaining exhibits, we can note the architectural members from the throne and altar of Apollo at Amyclae, Roman sculptures and mosaics with mythological themes, seascapes and portraits, etc.

p. 145
Laconian relief, probably depicting Menelaus and Helen (sixth century AD, Sparta Museum).

MYSTRAS

p. 146

Above: the Crucifixion, a wall-painting from the diakonikon of the church of the Peribleptos Monastery, fourteenth century.

Below: a relief with a double-headed eagle from the floor of Mystras Cathedral.

p. 147

The katholikon of the Monastery of Our Lady Queen of All, fifteenth century.

Mystras or Myzethras, clinging to the steep sides of Mt Taygetus, was the proud capital of the Despotate of the Morea. The strategic value of the site of the city had attracted the attention of the Franks at an early date, and in 1249 William II Villehardouin built on the summit of the hill the **castle** that still stands there today. In 1262, the castle was surrendered to the Byzantines and it soon became the focus around which the population of Sparta clustered. The new inhabitants walled their town, which they called **Pano Chora** ('upper town') and which lay outside the castle on the north side of the hill. There were two gates in the Byzantine walls: the **Nafplio Gate** to the north west and the **Monemvasia Gate** to the east. There was a main street from one gate to the other, passing through an open space on the north side which was the **main square** of the town, what the Byzantines called a *foro*. Construction work on the town was completed in the fourteenth century, by which time the buildings had spread down to the foot of the hill in what was called the **Kato Chora** or **Mesochora** ('lower' or 'inner' town). A third wall was built around this new quarter. In 1348, Mystras became the seat of the Despots of the Morea and was a place of great renown - until 1460, when it was taken by the Turks. In 1687, it passed into Venetian hands and flourished again, but in 1715 the Turks captured the city once more and it declined. In 1770 it suffered a disastrous fire.

In its days of glory, Mystras was one of the most power-

p. 148
Above: the east apse of Our Lady Queen of All, fifteenth century.

Below: the chapel of St George, owned privately by one of the noble families of Mystras.

ful administrative, commercial, intellectual and artistic centres of the Byzantine world, and it kept close ties with Constantinople. In the fifteenth century, Mystras was the home of the famous philosopher Gemistus Plethon, and throughout that century and the preceding one the city attracted many scholars and acquired many fine monuments. Most of those monuments have survived, and today Mystras gives us a good impression of what a Byzantine city must have been like.

The whole hillside is covered with ruined **houses**, with thick, solid walls often reinforced with towers so that the houses remind us of little fortresses. Among the many mansions are those of the Lascaris and Frangopoulos families. In the square of Pano Chora stand the imposing **palaces** of Mystras, which were constructed in three successive phases. The earliest palace building is that which stands to the east, built either by the Franks or the first Greek masters of the town. Shortly after 1348, when Mystras became the seat of the Catacuzene Despots, a new two-storey

building was constructed further to the north, with six rooms on each floor and a balcony on the north side. The continuous two-storey building on the west side of the square is the most recent, dating from after 1400. This was the monumental palace of the Palaeologue Despots, which was destroyed by fire shortly after the fall of the Despotate in 1460. The ground floor had eight sets of apartments, while the upper floor contained the throne-room, with wall-paintings and eight different fireplaces to provide heating.

The Byzantine churches of Mystras are especially interesting, and most of them have now been restored. The **Cathedral**, dedicated to St Demetrius, was originally built as a three-aisled church by the Metropolitan Bishop Eugenius (1263-1272). In 1286-1315, Metropolitan Bishop Nicephorus Moschopoulos added a vaulted narthex and a colonnade on the west side, while in the fifteenth century Metropolitan Bishop Matthew converted the church into a composite structure: at ground level it is a three-aisled basilica,

p. 149

Left: view of Mystras with the church of the Holy Wisdom at the centre, fourteenth century.

Right, above: the church of the Sts Theodore, thirteenth century.

Right, below: the church of the Perivleptos Monastery, fourteenth century.

but the roof is that of a cross-in-square church. Inside there are important wall-paintings from all the stages in the development of the Cathedral, and the buildings around the courtyard operate as a little **museum**. Vrondochiou Monastery consists of two churches, of the Sts Theodore and of Our Lady 'Hodeghetria', also known as 'Afentiko'. Building of the church of **Sts Theodore** began in 1290, when Daniil was abbot, and was completed in 1296 under Pachomius. The church is octagonal, with a later narthex. **'Afentiko'** was built by Pachomius in 1311-1322 and belongs to the composite type. This church is notable for the harmony of its proportions and for the outstanding wall-paintings which adorn its interior. In the vicinity of the palace, Manuel Catacuzene (1348-1383) built the *katholikon* of Zoodotos Monastery, which has been identified with the **church of the Holy Wisdom**, and also the *katholikon* of **Perivleptos Monastery** (both churches are of the cross-in-square type, with cupolas). Also of this architectural type is the small **church of Our Lady of the Annunciation** (late 14th century). The *katholikon* **of Pantanassa** ('Our Lady Queen of ALL') **Monastery** was built by master mason Ioannis Frangopoulos in 1428. It is interesting for its marked Western influence. The churches of **St Christopher** (late 14th century), **St Nicholas** (17th century) and **St George** can also be seen at Mystras.

p. 150

The Ascension, wall-painting from the sanctuary apse in Our Lady Queen of All, fifteenth century.

MONEMVASIA

Monemvasia stands at the foot of a steep rock which protrudes into the sea and is linked to land by only a narrow strip of land. This imposing place is a superb natural fortress, which is why, in the sixth century AD, the Lacedaemonians chose it as their refuge from the constant raids of the Arabs and Slavs. The new town grew into an important sea-faring power and one of the trading centres of the Byzantine Empire, and for many centuries it retained the privilege of self-government. In 1249, it was captured by William II Villehardouin after a siege lasting three years and despite the stout resistance of the townspeople, but in 1263 it had to be handed back to the Byzantine Emperor. When the rest of the Peloponnese succumbed to the Turks in 1460, Monemvasia managed to keep its liberty, and for four years was under the protection of Pope Pius

II. In 1464, it became Venetian, and went into decline. The Turks eventually took it in 1560 and kept it until 1690, after which it was in Venetian hands again from 1690 to 1715 and then occupied by the Turks until 1823.

From the modern village of Yefyra, on the mainland, there is no sign of Monemvasia at all; only the steep, forbidding cliff can be sean. We have to cross the narrow causeway and round the south-east corner of the rock before we can see the charming restored houses of the town. On the top of the rock is the **Upper town**. This is surrounded by a **wall** in rectangular layout, probably dating from the sixth century AD and later repaired by both the Byzantines and the Turks. The Upper Town was abandoned when Monemvasia was surrendered to Venice in 1690, and today only ruins of it have survived. However, the **church of the Holy Wisdom** (or of Our Lady 'Hodeghetria') has been preserved in good condition,

p. 151

The towering rock of Monemvasia and the narrow causeway that connects it to the mainland.

largely because the Turks converted it into a mosque. This is one of the finest octagonal churches to be seen anywhere in Greece, and the unusual care which was taken over its constructional details is testimony to the prosperity of Monemvasia in the mid-twelfth century. The exo-narthex of the church of the Holy Wisdom was added by the Venetians in 1600, and inside there are traces of wall-paintings dating from the seventeenth century.

Around the foot of the rock cluster the houses of the **Lower Town**, dating from the same period as the upper settlement. The Lower Town has been inhabited without interruption and was a major centre for seafaring activities. On three sides it is protected by **walls**, built by the Byzantines and extended under the Venetians and Turks. Today, the main **gate** into the town is on the west, which is where the main - commercial - street of Monemvasia begins. In the main square is the church of **Christ in Chains**, which seems to have been first constructed in the sixth century. At that time it was a wooden-roofed basilica, which the Venetians later reconstructed and to which they added a dome. The church was severely damaged in 1770, and in 1821 it was rebuilt again, to new plans. Inside, an important icon of the Crucifixion, dating from the fourteenth century, was kept until recently, and the icon of Christ in Chains can still be seen. Also in the Lower Town are the churches of **Our Lady 'Chrysafitissa', St Nicholas,** and **Our Lady of Crete (or 'Myrtidiotissa')**. Monemvasia, birthplace of the great modern Greek poet Yannis Ritsos, has been placed under a preservation order and attracts large numbers of visitors each year.

pp. 152-153
Views of the town and castle of Monemvasia. The houses of the Lower Town, huddled against the steep cliff and enclosed within fortifications, are a unique sight. Centre: the Byzantine church of the Holy Wisdom in the Upper Town.

YITHEIO - THE MANI
THE CAVE OF DIROS

We now cross the plain of Lakonia, and 46 km. to the south of Sparta come to the coastal town of Yitheio. **Yitheio** stands on a naturally amphitheatrical site at the foot of the hill called Koumaro or Larysio, and just off the coast is the islet of Cranae. The area was occupied in prehistoric times, and was a harbour and colony of the Phoenicians. In the historical period, it became the port and naval base of Sparta, and flourished under the Romans as a member of the Koinon of the Free Laconians. Traces of the ancient city have come to light to the north of the modern town.

The promontory of Cape Taenaron, between the Messenian and the Laconian Gulfs, is known as the **Mani** and is a place with a unique character and with features all its own in terms of its history, its architecture and the way of life of its people. The geographical factor has been of decisive importance in shaping the character of this area: most of the villages are built on the steep slopes of the southernmost extremities of the Taygetos range, where very little grows, water is scarce and access is extremely difficult. Nonetheless, the Mani has been inhabited since prehistoric times, and until the second century BC it was in the sphere of influence of Sparta. In 193 BC, the coastal cities of the area joined the Koinon of the Free

p. 154
Part of the town of Yitheio, on the southern edge of the plain of Lakonia.

p. 155
Vatheia, a typical village in the Mani.
Its striking tower-houses accommodated and protected the local people.

Laconians, detaching themselves from Sparta. In the Byzantine period, pirate raids forced the inhabitants to abandon their coastal settlements and retreat inland, to the mountain fastnesses of Taygetos. Until not long ago, it was believed that the Maniots had not adopted Christianity until the ninth century, but recent archaeological finds have disproved this view. **Early Christian basilicas** of the fifth and sixth centuries have come to light in many of the villages, and there are many **Byzantine churches** of later date in which marble architectural members, wall-paintings and portable icons of the greatest artistic value are to be seen. There are also numerous interesting **post-Byzantine churches** of the seventeenth and eighteenth centuries.

p. 156
Above: coastal village in the Mani.

Centre and below: views of the Diros caves, with superb combinations of stalactites and stalagmites.

When they took over the Peloponnese, the Franks built three strong **castles** to control the unruly Maniots: those of **Passava** near Yitheio, **Megali Maina**, and **Leftrou** (a corruption of Beaufort). But after the battle of Pelagonia, all three fortresses passed into the hands of the Maniots. In 1460, the Turks granted privileges to the Mani,

which did not stop the local people allying themselves with Venice. After 1715, the area continued to be self-governing, being obliged only to pay taxes to the Ottoman Empire. The Mani played a particularly important part in the Greek War of Independence, since its rough hills provided just the kind of safety needed for the preparation of military operations. The Maniots distinguished themselves in the fighting in the Peloponnese, but they were also represented in the battles which took place elsewhere. Many of the Maniot villages are severely depopulated nowadays. Even so, we can discern a

tough, austere nature which reminds us of the ancient Laconians who were the forebears of these people. For many centuries, the inaccessible mountains of the Mani hid a truculent people, whose houses - for that reason - were more like fortresses than residences. The **tower-houses** of the Byzantine period, with their scant windows and their thick stone walls, were the foundations of Maniot architecture, and many fine examples of them can still be seen today. The way of life of the Maniots continues to be as conservative and isolationist as their architecture. At the entrance to the Mani is **Areo-polis**, which is a good starting-point for a tour of the villages of the **Mesa Mani**, towards the tip of the promontary, and to the less barren landscapes of the **Exo Mani**, further north on the Messenian side. At Diros, 12 km. from Areopolis, are three of the most impressive cavern lakes in Europe, known as Glyfada, Alepotrypa and Katafigi. A river runs through all three of the caves, which are visited by boat. The **Alepotripa cave**, which archaeological finds show was inhabited in Neolithic times, is of particular interest. The Alepotripa cave has an ingenious **museum** with finds from the area.

p. 157

Yitheio harbour. Traces of Roman buildings (theatre, baths, aqueduct, temple of the Caesars) have come to light to the north of the town.

KALAMATA

Kalamata, capital of the Prefecture of Messinia, stands at the head of the Messenian Gulf, in the verdant plain of the river Nedon. In antiquity, the site was occupied by the city of Pharae. Between the eighth century BC and the battle of Leuctra in 371 BC, Pharae was under the domination of Sparta. Beneath the modern city are the foundations of houses dating from between the eighth century BC and the Roman period. The modern name of Kalamata was given to the city by the Byzantines, who built a little fortress on the ancient acropolis. In 1208, a new **castle** was constructed by William de Villehardouin, who was born in Kala-

p. 158
Partial view of Kalamata harbour. There is a fine view over the plain of Messinia from the castle, the highest point in the town.

mata and always took a particular interest in the city. Most of the castle was demolished by the Venetians in 1685 and then reconstructed. To the north of the castle, the Byzantine church of **Our Lady 'Kalomata'** (13th century) has survived, while at the entrance to the castle a modern amphitheatre is used for artistic events.

In the market area of Kalamata is the **church of the Holy Apostles**, where on 23 March 1823 a church service marked the official commencement of the Greek War of Independence. The east part of the church was built late in the twelfth or early in the thirteenth century in the cross-in-square type with a dome, while during the first period of Venetian rule a

single-aisled church with a cupola and a bell-tower was added to the west.

Kalamata has a **library**, founded in 1933, and an **Archaeological Museum** with finds dating from between antiquity and the nineteenth century. Although the city was severely damaged by an earthquake in 1986, it is attractively laid out and has an excellent beach.

ANCIENT MESSENE

A ncient Messene, near the modern village of Mavromati, is one of the most important archaeological sites to be seen anywhere in Greece. The city was the capital of the people of Messenia when, in the fourth century BC, they were finally liberated after centuries of exile as refugees. The Messenians were among the pre-Doric Greek tribes, who were subdued by Sparta after the Dorian invasion. As early as the second half of the eighth century BC the Spartans embarked on a series of campaigns called the 'Messenian wars' whose purpose was to conquer Messenia. After their defeat, the Messenians were initially reduced to a state of slavery, later becoming helots. The last conflict between Sparta and Messenia took place early in the fifth century BC, and after it, with the help of Athens, some of the Messenians managed to escape to Naupactus; during the Peloponnesian War, they took the side of Athens. When hostilities were over, the Spartans threw themselves into an even more merciless pursuit of these Messenians, who were forced to leave Naupactus and seek refuge as far

away as North Africa and Sicily. The restoration of Messenia was not effected until the time of Epaminondas of Thebes, who defeated Sparta at the battle of Leuctra in 371 BC and founded the city of Messene as part of his attempt to ensure that Spartan expansionism was never a threat again. The Messenians were supported by Philip II of Macedon, but Alexander the Great established a tyranny in their state. In 191-182 BC, Messene was a member of the Achaean League, coming under Roman control in 146 BC. Under the Romans, the city flourished, a state of affairs which lasted until 395 BC, when the area was devastated by Alaric.

Ancient Messene stands in the foothills of **Mt Ithome**, where the **acropolis** of the ancient city was located and which was the centre of the cult of Zeus Ithomatas. The city was surrounded by **walls** built in the third century BC, some sections of which have survived. They were among the few defensive structures in Greece to have been constructed entirely in stone.

The first building we come to in the archaeological site is the **theatre**, probably dating from the time when the city was founded. Ancient Messene was laid out on the Hippodamian system.

p. 159
A traditional festival in Kalamata.

In the **Agora** of Messene, the **spring of Arsinoe, colonnades, water tanks** and a **sanctuary of Demeter** have been excavated, the latter having been in use from the seventh to the fourth centuries BC. The most important of the Messenian sanctuaries was that **dedicated to Asclepius**. It was founded in the Hellenistic period in an attempt to accentuate the importance of the Messenian people, given that in Messenia Asclepius was more of a political than a religious figure and was worshipped as a local hero. In the **temple of Asclepius** itself, the goddess Messene, a personification of the city, was worshipped down to Roman times. In the cella of the Doric peripteral temple was a statue of Messene, with paintings showing the history of the city in the *opisthodomos*.

To the south of the **east monumental gateway** into the sanctuary was the **Bouleuterium**, where the community of the Messenians met in session, and to the north was a small **Odeum**, also used as a meeting-place for the assembly. On one side of the north gateway, archaeologists have excavated the **Caesareum** or **Sebasteum**, where the Roman Emperors were worshipped, and on the other is **house H**, where there were statues of Machaon and Podalerius, sons of Asclepius who were themselves renowned physicians during the Trojan War. The statues were by the famous Messenian sculptor Damophon, who was also responsible for a line of statues in the buildings on the west side of the Asclepium. To the south west of the Asclepium, excavations have revealed the city **Stadium** and its Gymnasium. Three festivals were held in the Stadium each year: the Asclepeia, the Ithomaea and, in Roman times, the Caesarea. Around three sides of the running-track and the curved end of the stadium were the Doric colonnades of the **Gymnasium**, whose columns were discovered upright, in their proper positions.

In the square of the pretty nearby village of Mavromati, the local people still use a fountain which predates the founding of Messene and was called **Clepsydra**. The river deity Achelous was worshipped at the Clepsydra spring from the seventh to the fourth century BC.

p. 161
View of the pretty town of Pylos, on the slopes of Ayios Nikolaos hill.

THE PYLOS AREA

On the south-west coast of the Peloponnese is the Bay of Navarino, where the modern town of Pylos stands. The area is of the greatest historical interest, and has been inhabited without interruption since prehistoric times. On the north side of Navarino Bay, on the shore of the inlet called **Voidokilia**, is a cave in which traces of human habitation in Palaeolithic times have been found, and many sites occupied in the Neolithic and Early Bronze Ages have been excavated in the area. However, we can deduce from the wealth of highly important finds from the vicinity of Pylos that the area reached the height of its power and influence in the Mycenean period.

The most important discovery of all, of course - made by Carl Blegen and K. Kourouniotis in 1939 - is the **Palace of Nestor**, on the hill of Ano Englianos, 17 km. to the north of Pylos. Traditionally, the area was said to have been first inhabited by Neleus, who was forced to leave his

birthplace of Iolcus when he quarrelled with his brother Peleus. Nestor, king of Pylus and second most senior commander in the Trojan expedition, was the son of Neleus.

The site at Englianos hill was occupied early in the Bronze Age, and the prosperity of the palace was at its greatest from 1400 to 1200 BC. Unlike the other Mycenean sites, the acropolis of Englianos was not fortified, a feature in which a similarity to the undefended Minoan palaces can be seen. Further Minoan influence has been detected in the way in which the palace complex was constructed. The palace was entered from the south, through a **gateway** of the Minoan type to the left of which was the **Archive Room**. Here the archaeologists discovered a large number of terracotta plaques with inscriptions in Linear B script relating to the palace accounts.

On the right of the gateway was a tower-like structure which was probably used as a **guard-post**, while the **main courtyard** of the palace lay to the north. Two rooms to the west of the courtyard were used as a **waiting-room** and as a **food store**. The courtyard led to a megaron in three parts, consisting of a distyle portico, a vestibule and a chamber. In the chamber, surrounded by four

columns, was a circular hearth with ornamentation, the largest and most monumental found to date. The surround of the hearth was ornamented with painted running spirals, with a flame motif on the edge. The ornamentation of the floor was arranged in squares, in one of which is a representation of an octopus, while on the walls were paintings (a lyre-player with a bird, feathered griffons and lions). The position of the throne, against the east wall, can also be seen in the chamber. The megaron was surrounded by **storerooms** for olive oil, wine and wool, as we can tell from the numerous Linear B inscriptions. Among the storerooms are the remains of two **staircases** which led to the upper floor of the palace. To the east of the complex was the **queen's apartment**, with a small, circular clay hearth in the centre of the floor and paintings on the walls (wingless griffons and lions). To the north was the **bath chamber**, in which a terracotta bath has survived. To the east were **two courtyards**; further in this direction there was a **wine-store** (to the north) and a **workshop** or **armoury** (to the south), in which there was also a **shrine**. To the west of the palace, archaeologists have uncovered the **old palace of Pylus**, consisting of an antechamber and the main megaron

pp. 162-163

Reconstructions of Nestor's Palace near Pylos: left, the inner courtyard; right, the throne-room.

(14th-13th century BC). Many of the finds from the palace of Nestor and the Pylos area in general are housed in the **Museum** of **Chora Trifyllias**, 4 km. to the north of Englianos hill. In the **first room** is a rich collection of Mycenean pottery, together with gold artefacts found in tombs. Note the three gold hats and the large gold diadem from the three tholos tombs found at Peristeria. The **second** and **third rooms** contain finds from the palace of Nestor: storage vessels, the moulds for making the plaques with the Linear B inscriptions, potteries, fragments of wall-paintings and reconstructions of what the paintings must have looked like.

p. 164

An earthenware Mycenaean ewer from the area around Pylos.

p. 165

The Bourtzi at Methoni castle, sixteenth century.

Some time around 1200 BC, the palace of Nestor was destroyed by fire, which brought cultural development in the area to an abrupt halt. The site continued to be occupied down to the Geometric period, while Classical Pylus occupied the site of Coryphasium, further to the south. The **promontory of Coryphasium**, on the shore of Navarino Bay, was fortified in 425 BC, during the Peloponnesian War. On the island of Sphakteria, out in the bay itself, a force of Spartans was besieged by Athenian troops and eventually surrendered, after putting up stout resistance.

In 1278, the Franks built a castle - known as **Palaiokastro** or **Palaionavarino** - on the site once occupied by ancient Pylus.

Navarino Bay, where the modern town stands, is almost completely enclosed on its west side by the island of **Sphakteria**; the bay is entered through narrow channels to the north and south of the island. The north channel was guarded by Paliokastro, while on the mainland coast above the south channel the Turks started work in 1573 - shortly after their defeat in the sea-battle of Lepanto - on the castle of **Niokastro**. This is one of the best-preserved castles in Greece. Inside it is the church of the **Transfiguration of Our Lord**, in the Gothic style. In 1827, the battle of Navarino, with the Turks facing the united fleets of France, Britain and Russia, was fought in the bay. The victory, after a battle lasting only four hours, of admirals de Rigny, Codrington and Heiden, marked the approach of liberation for Greece. Monuments to the French and Russian sailors who fell in the battle have been erected on Sphakteria.

Modern Pylos was built in the period after 1829 to plans by the French General Maison. This attractive town stands on an amphitheatrical site on the hill of Ayios Nikolaos. In the pretty, tree-shaded **Square of the Three Admirals** is a monument depicting the victors of the battle of Navarino. Also to be seen in Pylos is the house **of Olympic medallist Kostas Tsiklitiras** (1912), and there is a **museum** (the **Antonopouleio**) with a collection covering the period from the Neolithic era to Roman times.

METHONI - KORONI

A t the south-west extremity of the Peloponnese is **Methoni**, a harbour of great strategic significance. In earlier times, the town was called Pedasus, taking the name of Methone or Mothone after the first Messenian War. From the time of the second Messenian War down to the fourth century BC it was in the hands of Nafplio, after which it was fortified and became independent. Under Byzantium, the town was wealthy, and in 1206 it passed into the hands of Venice, which reconstructed the walls using ancient materials. The **Venetian castle** is separated from the town by a **moat** on which additional fortifying work was done during the second period of Venetian rule, from 1686 to 1715. This is also the date of the monumental **gate** we see today, while the arched bridge linking the castle with the town was built by General

p. 166
Views of Methoni
and Koroni
(below).

Maison's French soldiers in 1828. The walls run along all three of the sides of the castle washed by the sea, ending in an imposing gateway on the south side. From there, a bridge links the castle to the **Bourtzi**, an octagonal tower standing on a tiny islet, built in the sixteenth century by the Turks. The castle of Methoni fell to the Turks in 1500, to the Venetians in 1686 and to the Turks again in 1715. In 1828 it was liberated by the French expeditionary force under General Maison.

Koroni, another town with a famous Venetian castle, stands on a promontory 50 km. to the south of Kalamata. The Venetians occupied the area in 1206, after driving out Geoffrey de Villehardouin. In 1500, after the local people rose in revolt, the castle was surrendered to the Turks, returning to Venetian hands in 1689. The Turks recaptured it in 1715 and in 1828 it was liberated by General Maison. Inside the castle of Koroni is a Byzantine church of the Holy Wisdom.

p. 167

The octagonal sixteenth-century tower called the Bourtzi at Methoni.

THESSALY

p. 168
Landscapes in
Thessaly.

Thessaly is in the centre of mainland Greece, bordering on Epirus and Macedonia to the west and north and on the south with the region of Central Greece. To the east, it is washed by the Aegean, which forms the Pagasitic Gulf in the Prefecture of Magnisia. Most of Thessaly consists of the plain by the same name, one of the most fertile parts of Greece, where cereals and cotton are the main crops. The plain of Thessaly is surrounded by the mountain massifs of Ossa, Pelion, Olympus and Othrys. On the south side of Mt Olympus is the Vale of Tempe, an idyllic and thickly-wooded spot. The river Peneios, in whose upper basin is the Meteora district (see the relevant entry), runs through the Vale of Tempe.

We can conclude from the information supplied by the historian Thucydides that the first Thessalians penetrated into the area that bears their name shortly after the Trojan War, moving on from their earlier settlements in Thesprotia. The subjugation of Thessaly by these new tribes was complete by about the ninth century BC. The land they had conquered was divided into four tribal states (Histaeotis, Thessaliotis, Pelasgiotis and Phthiotis), which in the seventh century BC formed an alliance and based their military power on strong forces of cavalry. The Thessalians, who had the largest army in

VOLOS - PAGASAE - DEMETRIAS

At the head of the Pagasitic Gulf and the foot of Mt Pelion is **Volos**, one of the most important harbours of central Greece. The city has been identified with prehistoric **Iolcus**, where Pelias, according to the traditions, was king. Pelias' brother Aeson, who had been excluded from power, feared for the life of his son Jason, and so sent him up on to Mt Pelion to live with Chiron, the wise Centaur. As Jason was making his way back to Iolcus, he lost one of his sandals, thus confirming an oracle which said that Pelias should fear the menace represented by 'the man with one sandal'. Pelias promised his nephew succession to the throne if he could bring back the Golden Fleece from Colchis. Jason successfully completed this hazardous mission (the voyage of the *Argo*), and returned with Medea as his wife. Pelias himself met a frightful end, since Medea plotted to have him order himself dismembered and boiled, in the hope that this would restore his youth. At the spot called Pefkakia near modern Volos is a little harbour where, it is believed, the *Argo*, Jason's ship, was built, while various views have been expressed as to the possible position of ancient Iolcus. The most likely of these identifies the palace of Pelias with a **Mycenean megaron** discovered in Volos town itself, beneath the medieval castle. Excavations revealed three successive phases in the history of the palace (15th, 14th and 13th centuries BC), and

p. 170

The spreading plain of Thessaly is surrounded by the highest mountains in Greece, creating striking contrasts of landscape.

◄ *p. 169*

Meteora: the gigantic outcrops of stone on the north-west edge of the plain of Thessaly are a unique natural phenomenon.

the Greek world at the time, bore the brunt of the operations of the First Sacred War of 600 BC (see Delphi). During the Persian Wars, Thessaly medized, and the area was neutral during the Peloponnesian War. In the meantime, the Aleuad dynasty of Larisa had been the leading force in political affairs, with the exception of a short period in the fourth century BC when the tyrant Jason of Pherae was in the ascendant. In 352 BC, Thessaly was conquered by Philip II of Macedon. In the time of his successor Philip V, the area was ravaged by the Romans, and after 146 BC it was a Roman province. In Byzantine times, Thessaly was repeatedly raided: by the Goths (4th-5th century AD), the Huns (6th century), the Slavs (6th-7th century), the Bulgars (7th-10th century) and the Normans (11th century). When Constantinople fell to the Franks in 1204, Thessaly passed through the hands of the Venetians, Boniface of Montserrat, the Despotate of Epirus and the Empire of Nicaea before full Byzantine control was restored. In 1420 it was taken by the Turks, who occupied it until annexation by Greece in 1881.

brought important finds to light. At Kalpakli, a **Mycenean tholos tomb** of 1400 BC yielded excellent funerary offerings (now in Athens Archaeological Museum) which seem to have been connected with the palace of Iolcus.

In the historical period, Iolcus entered a period of prosperity, but in the fourth century BC it was overshadowed by the growth of the nearby **city of Pagasae**. In the Hellenistic period, Demetrius Poliorcetes founded **Demetrias** (294 BC) on the site of Pagasae. The site of Demetrias has yielded a **fortified precinct** with a circumference of about eight km., into which had been incorporated painted funerary *stelae* of the third century BC, of the greatest artistic value. Remains have also survived of the city's **theatre**, of its **agora**, of what is known as the **palace of Demetrius** and of some

sections of a Roman **aqueduct**.

In the Byzantine period, Iolcus became known as Golos (hence Volos), and it was an important fortified town. In 1423 it was taken by the Turks, and the Christian population was driven up on to Mt Pelion. During the War of Independence of 1821, Volos and Pelion fought hard for their freedom, which did not come until 1881 with the annexation of the whole of Thessaly.

The modern city was built in the mid-nineteenth century and is a typical large Greek town. The harbour is a fine place for a romantic stroll, as is the suburb of Ano Volos, a largely traditional settlement on a naturally amphitheatrical site. Volos has an **Archaeological Museum** which is interesting as much for the wealth and variety of its exhibits as for the original

p. 171
View of the city of Volos on the Pagasitic Gulf, with the church of St Constantine.

and instructive manner in which they are laid out. Two rooms in the Museum are given over to the finds from the Palaeolithic sites on the banks of the River Peneios and from the important Neolithic settlements of Dimini and Sesklo (see below). Of particular interest are the painted funerary *stelae* found in the walls of Demetrias, and the relief funerary *stelae* found elsewhere in Thessaly (dating from the 5th century BC to the Roman period).

SESKLO - DIMINI

Long before the founding of Iolcus, there were two important settlements in the vicinity of Volos: Sesklo and Dimini, traces of which can still be seen today. **Sesklo** seems to have been inhabited first in about the middle of the seventh millenium BC, and it grew in the Middle Neolithic period (5th millenium BC) into a town of unprecedented size for the time. The **houses** of the settlement had stone foundations and walls of mud-brick, and the inhabitants supported themselves by farming and cottage industry. The art of pottery was very well-developed, as can be seen in the important vases with careful painted designs which were

p. 172
Neolithic vessels from Dimini in Thessaly and Lianokladi near Lamia (National Archaeological Museum, Athens).

found in large quantities, notably in the so-called **potter's house**. The acropolis of Sesklo had a walled precinct at the centre of which stood a building of the *megaron* type. In the Late Neolithic period (4th millenium BC), the large town around the acropolis was abandoned. A new precinct was constructed on the acropolis, together with a new **megaron** consisting of three rooms (the portico, the domus and the chamber). Adjacent to this main megaron was a second one, in a similar architectural form. On the plain around the acropolis have been found numerous **tombs** dating from the Bronze Age.

Dimini was founded in the Late Neolithic period and is unique in being surrounded by **six precincts** arranged in pairs, which some scholars have interpreted as fortifications and others as retaining walls. The two innermost walls marked out the main **square**, around which were the **houses** of the town and the **cottage industry buildings** (storerooms, workshops where cloth was woven, tool-shops, a pottery kiln). In the centre of the square, archaeologists have excavated the **me-garon** of Dimini, a building with three rooms which was still inhabited by a farming family down to the early third millennium BC, by which time the rest of the town had been abandoned. In the Middle Helladic period, a **cemetery** of shaft tombs was located here, and in Mycenean times a new town grew up to the south-east of the Neolithic acropolis. To this belong two **Mycenean tholos tombs** found at Dimini (14th-13th century BC). The Mycenean settlement was laid waste late in the twelfth century BC.

PELION

The massif of Mt Pelion occupies the eastern part of the Prefecture of Magnesia, starting to the north of Volos and ending far to its south, in a promontory that protrudes into the Pagasitic Gulf.

The dense, wild vegetation of the mountain, its steep, windy peaks and its water-rich forests inspired the ancient Greeks at an early date, and led their imagination into the creation of a whole series of fascinating myths. This inaccessible mountain, say the traditions, was the home of the Centaurs, monstrous beasts whose bodies were half-equine and half-human. They were led by the wise Centaur Chiron, who was responsible for initiating the god Asclepius, Achilles, Jason and many other mortals and heroes into the secrets of knowledge. It was on Pelion, too, that the mythical marriage of Peleus (not to be confused with Pelias) and Thetis took place, attended by all the gods of Olympus. During the wedding ceremony, the animal instincts of the Centaurs drove them to attack the women of the Lapiths, one of the local tribes. A fight broke out between the gods and the Centaurs - the Battle of the Centaurs, a subject which inspired many of the artists of antiquity.

Most of the villages of Mt Pelion developed high up in the hills dur-

p. 173

Milies, Mt Pelion: the station.

ing the Hellenistic period, when the coastal towns had to be abandoned because of the growth of Demetrias and the Macedonian control over it. In the seventh and eighth centuries AD, the area was largely depopulated, and it was not until the thirteenth century that life returned, mostly in the form of monastic communities and small villages which soon came under the sway of the Venetians.

The oldest villages to be seen today date back to Turkish times, after 1423, and flourished in the Middle Ages because of the privileges which they were able to wring out of the conquerors.

After the mid-eighteenth century, the development of the area was closely connected with the silk industry and with sea-faring. This prosperity was accompanied by an unusually vigorous trend towards building, the traces of which can still be seen today in such of the mansions of Mt Pelion as have survived. There was much progress in learning, too, and many of the schools of the period have survived (the 'Greek Museum' of Zagora, the 'Lyceum' of Milies, the schools in Makrynitsa, Portaria and elsewhere). In the Greek War of Independence, the villages of Pelion fought hard, under the leadership of Anthimos Gazis and the many members of the Philike Etaireia.

The area was liberated in 1881, and is today under a general preservation order, constituting a major tourist attraction during the winter months as well as the summer.

pp. 174-175
Landscapes on Mt Pelion: villages clinging to steep cliffs surrounded by the dense forests in which, accordance to ancient traditions, lived the mythical beasts called Centaurs.

LARISA

Larisa, chief town of the Prefecture of the same name, stands almost in the centre of the Plain of Thessaly, on the right bank of the river Peneios. Tradition relates that it was founded by the Pelasgians in the second millenium BC. Around 1100 BC, it became the new home for the Thessalian tribes who had been driven south (from Thesprotia) by the Dorian invasion. In the time of the Persian Wars, Larisa signed a peace treaty with Xerxes, the Persian king, and during the fifth century BC it flourished under the dynasty of the Aleuad family. In 369 BC it came under Macedonian sovereignty, and in 146 under the Romans. In the thirteenth century AD, the Despotate of Epirus ruled Larisa, and in 1396 it was captured by the Turks. Union with the Greek state came in 1882.

On a low hill towards the north side of the town is the **Cathedral**, which occupies a site on which traces of the ancient **acropolis**, a **temple of Athena** and a **Hellenistic theatre** have come to light. Remains have also been discovered of the **ancient Agora**, while a **medieval castle** stands on the acropolis hill and a **Byzantine bridge** spans the River Peneios. In the centre of Larisa, the **Archaeological Museum** is housed in a Turkish mosque; it has finds dating from between the Palaeolithic era (banks of the Peneios) and the Byzantine period. Larisa is today a large city and one of the agricultural as well as intellectual centres of central Greece, apart from being an important junction on the public transport network.

TRIKALA –
OUR LADY OF PORTA

Trikala, chief town of the Prefecture by the same name, stands on the site of ancient Trikke, which took its name from a nymph who in mythology was a daughter of the river-god Peneus. Trikke was a centre for the cult of Asclepius, whose worship spread from there to the rest of Greece. There is a tradition that the healer-god was born in Trikke, and that he built his own temple. Traces of the **Asclepium** (2nd century BC) have come to light close to the main square of the modern town. On the hill occupied by the ancient **acropolis** are some parts of a **medieval castle**. Also to be seen are the surviving mansions of the **Varousi** quarter, which developed in the eighteenth and nineteenth centuries outside the castle walls.

Near the church of St Constantine, the mosque called the **Kursum çami**, built in 1550 by the architect Sinan, one of the most famous of his time, has been reconstructed. Very close to Trikala, in a ravine which marks the border between Thessaly and Epirus, is the village of Porta, near which the monastery of **Our Lady of Porta** was built in 1283. The founder was the Sebastocrator John Ducas, son of Despot Michael II of Epirus. In architectural terms, the monastery is a copy of the church of Kato Panayia which Michael had erected in Arta in 1236-1271: it is a three-aisled cruciform-roofed church, inside which wall-paintings of the thirteenth, fifteenth and seventeenth centuries have survived.

pp. 176-177
The river Peneios flows through the Tempi gorge, amid one of the finest landscapes in Thessaly.

KALABAKA - METEORA

p. 178
Above: the Monastery of the Transfiguration or Great Meteoron, fourteenth century.

K alabaka, known in Byzantine times as Stagi, is a little town which is the starting-point for a visit to the Meteora. Kalabaka itself has a fourteenth-century **cathedral church** whose wall-paintings were executed in 1573 by the monk Neophytos, son of the painter Theophanis.

The **Meteora** is a group of steep, towering rocks in the centre of the Plain of Thessaly. This unique geological phenomenon was created by a series of upheavals in the earth's crust, and the landscape is of unique interest, especially when seen in conjunction with the monasteries which perch on top of the rocks. The untrodden rocky peaks of the Meteora seem to have attracted the interest of hermits as far back as the mid-eleventh century. A century later, the independent ascetics formed the *skete* of Stagi, called **Our Lady of Doupiani**, and the first monasteries of the Meteora were built in the fourteenth century.

Before long, the Meteora had developed into a major centre of monasticism, second only to Mt Athos itself. At this time, the Monastery of **Ipapanti** (1366) was built by the priest-monk Hieronymus and the Monastery of the **Transfiguration**, or Great Meteoron, by the Blessed Athanasius of Meteora (1348). The Blessed Athanasius, an eminent ascetic of great repute, composed the first regulations of the monastery, which served as a model for all the later foundations in the Meteora. The original church of the Monastery of the Transfiguration was constructed by

◀ p. 179
Rousanou Monastery, fifteenth/sixteenth century.

*p. 180
View of Mt Olympus. On the summit of the highest mountain in Greece snow lies all the year round.*

*p. 181
Above: Rousanou Monastery, fifteenth/sixteenth century.
Below: the Monastery of St Stephen, sixteenth century.*

the monk Joasaph, and has interesting wall-paintings of 1487. After a period of decline, the monastic centre began to flourish once again in the sixteenth century. In 1544/5, a new and more magnificent church was built at the Great Meteoron, in the Athonite architectural type. In 1552, when Symeon was abbot, the paintings of the monastery *katholikon* were executed. These works, which have survived down to the present day, are fine examples of the Cretan School of icon-painting. On a rock close to the Great Meteoron, the ascetic **Barlaam** founded the monastery which bears his name in the mid-fourteenth century. It was reconstructed in 1545, in the Athonite style, by the monks Theophanis and Nektarios, brothers from Ioannina. The main church of the monastery was dedicated to All Saints, and in 1548 it was ornamented with wall-paintings by the famous artist Frangos Katelanos of Thebes. The *lite* was decorated in 1566, with paintings by the brothers Yeorgios and Frangos Kontaris, also of Thebes.

The **monastery of St Nicholas 'Anapafsas'**, the closest to the village of Kastraki, was founded in the fourteenth century and renovated around 1500 by Dionysios, Bishop of Larisa, and the priest-monk Nikanoras. Inside the main church, which is a simple vaulted building with a cupola, are superb wall-paintings of 1527 by the Cretan artist Theophanis Strelitzas Bathas.

Rousanou Monastery was first constructed in the fourteenth or fifteenth century, and a new main church was built in 1527-1529 by the brothers Joasaph and Maximos of Ioannina. The wall-paintings inside the main church were executed in 1560, but the name of the artist - who was of the Cretan School - has not come down to us.

On the south-east side of the Meteora are two more important monasteries, those of the **Holy Trinity** (1438) and **St Stephen**, which today houses a community of nuns. Apart from the large monasteries which have survived in good condition, there are also many ruins of other churches which give some idea of the importance of the area and do much to transport the visitor back into the atmosphere of Byzantium.

MT OLYMPUS

Mt Olympus, highest of the Greek mountains at 2,917 metres, is the place which the twelve gods of the Greek Pantheon chose as their residence. With its majestic gorges, steep cliffs and forests of oak, beech and pine, it will delight even the most demanding visitor. Since 1938, Mt Olympus has been a National Park: one of Greece's finest. On its slopes grow some of the most ancient species of plant to be found in Europe, and the fauna is also notable, with the golden eagle as the most characteristic species.

THE SPORADES

The Sporades is the name given to the group of islands which lie to the north- east of Euboea and the south-east of Magnesia in Thessaly. Skiathos, Skopelos and Alonnisos belong administratively to Thessaly, while Skyros is part of the Prefecture of Euboea.

Skiathos, home of the well-known Greek writer Alexandros Papadiamandis, is now developing into a cosmopolitan holiday resort, thanks to its superb beaches. The ancient city of Sciathus was founded in the late sixth or early fifth century BC, and in 478 BC became part of the Athenian League. In 404 BC, after the Peloponnesian War, it became a Spartan possession, and in 378 BC was liberated by the Athenian general Chabrias. In 338 it was taken by Philip II of Macedon, and in 146 by the Romans; in 42 BC, they gave it to Athens, which kept the island as a dependency until the third century AD. In 1207 Skiathos was taken by the Venetians and in 1276 by the Byzantines, who built the castle which can still be seen in the north of the island. After a second period of Venetian rule, lasting from 1459 to 1540, Skiathos became a Turkish possession until liberation in 1830. Apart from the **castle**, the sights of Skiathos town today include the Venetian fortress of the **Bourtzi** (1270) and the **house of Alexandros Papadiamandis**, which operates as a museum. Around the island, and inside the castle in particular, there are numerous interesting **churches**, most of

p. 182
The pretty chapel of Our Lady adorns the west side of Skopelos harbour.

p. 183
The main village of Skopelos, on a naturally amphitheatrical site. At the top are the ruins of a thirteenth-century Venetian castle.

them dating from between the seventeenth and the nineteenth centuries.

Skopelos is the largest island in the Sporades group and, thanks to its abundant greenery and excellent beaches, one of the most beautiful islands in the Aegean. In antiquity, the island was called Peparethus, and it seems to have been inhabited as far back as prehistoric times, to judge from the **Mycenean tholos tomb of Staphylus** on the bay by the same name. In 700 BC, it became a colony of Chalcis, and in 340 BC passed into Macedonian control. Under the Byzantines, Skopelos was a place of exile. In 1204 it was annexed by the Duchy of Naxos. Between 1453 and 1538, the island was ruled by a Venetian provincial governor, after which the Turks took it and held it until liberation in 1821. The town of Skopelos, standing on a naturally amphitheatrical site on a hillside, is a place of unique beauty. On top of the hill are some remains of a thirteenth-century **Venetian castle**. The island can boast a total of 360 **churches**, of which the most notable are those of **Our Lady** 'Panayitsa', St Nicholas, and the Annunciation.

pp. 184-185
Skiathos: the main village of the island and its quiet beaches attract large numbers of visitors during the summer months.

Alonnisos is a primarily mountainous island. The chief village is **Patitiri**, by the sea, which gained in importance after 1965, when a devastating earthquake forced the islanders to abandon the earlier settlement higher up in the hills. All around Alonnisos are little islets (Kyra Panayia, Youra, Piperi, Skantzoura, Psathoura, Peristera and others), the sea off which has yielded a **fifth century BC shipwreck**, the earliest yet found. Among the notable monuments of the island is the Byzantine **church of Our Lady**, which has very fine wall-paintings.

Skyros is the most southerly island in the Sporades group. It is connected with the mythical hero Achilles, since this is said to be the island to which he fled so as to avoid taking part in the Trojan War. At Achilleio Bay, archaeologists have excavated a cave with Palaeolithic finds, together with a Neolithic settlement of the fifth millenium BC. In the historical period, Skyros was dominated by the Athenians (468 BC), the Macedonians (332 BC), and the Romans, who gave the island back to Athens in 196 BC. In medieval times, it was controlled by the Franks and the Venetians, being captured by the Turks in 1538. Liberation came in 1829. The sights of Skyros include a **Venetian castle** on the site of the ancient acropolis, and the Byzantine churches of **St George 'Skyrianos'** (10th century) and the **Dormition of the Virgin** (9th century). The unique residential architecture and the interior decoration of the houses, with the excellent locally-made furniture, are of particular interest.

p. 186

Above: the Kaloyeriko bridge, one of the best-preserved in Epirus, in the central Zagori villages.

Below: metal jug from Epirus (Ioannina Museum).

EPIRUS

Epirus is the name given to the north-west part of Greece, stretching from the peaks of the Pindus range to the coast of the Ionian Sea. To the north, it borders on Albania, to the east with the geographical region of Macedonia, and to the south-east with Central Greece and Thessaly. The west coast of Epirus is washed by the Ionian Sea, while the Ambracian Gulf lies to the south. The entire area is occupied by the Pindus range and its offshoots, making it an almost wholly mountainous part of the country (highest peak: Smolikas, 2687 m.). The only low-lying districts are to be found around the towns of Ioannina and Arta, but the abundant rainfall ensures the whole area of rich vegetation, especially in the valleys of the rivers (the Arachthos, the Louros, the Thyamis or Kalamas, the Acheron, the Aoos and the Voidomatis). Even so, the rocky peaks of the mountains in the hinterland are barren and sparsely-populated - indeed, the density of population in Epirus is lower than in any other part of Greece.

Epirus has been shown by the finds in Asprochaliko cave by the river Louros to have been inhabited in the Palaeolithic era. Inhabitation was continuous, with the first Greek tribes of the Thesprotians, the Molossians and

◄ p. 187

Ioannina: the Aslan Mosque, now housing the Hisrorial and Folklore Museum.

p. 188

Landscape in the Zagori villages: swift-running streams, dense greenery, and high mountains.

the Chaones settling in the area around 2000 BC. In the late ninth century BC, Corinth set up its colonies of Ambracia and Epidamnus, importing into Epirus some of the characteristics of southern Greece. Down to the fifth century BC, Epirus was ruled by the Thesprotians, but after that time the Molossians began to gain in power, and the period of their hegemony began with king Tharypas. In the fourth century BC, king Arybas married his niece Olympias to Philip II of Macedon, thus inaugurating friendly relationships with the strong and adjacent kingdom. The third century was dominated by the dynamic personality of king Pyrrhus of Epirus, who in 280 BC campaigned against the Romans but was ultimately defeated after an impres-sive series of victories. In 168 BC, the Romans occupied Epirus, where they found some 70 cities to destroy. After the triumph of Octavian at Actium in 31 BC, most of the inhabitants were forced to settle in the new city of Nicopolis which he founded. Between the fourth and the twelfth centuries AD, Epirus suffered from the incursions of Goths, Slavs and Normans. The Despotate of Epirus was founded in 1204, by Michael Comnenus Ducas, and the area flourished until the arrival of the Turks in 1430. In the time of the Greek War of Independence, most of the villages of Epirus fought hard for their freedom, but it was not until 1881 that a small part of the region was liberated, the remained following in 1912-13 during the Balkan Wars.

IOANNINA - PERAMA

Ioannina is the chief town of the Prefecture by the same name, and it stands on the shores of Lake Pambotis. The historian Procopius tells us it was founded in 527 AD by the Emperor Justinian. In Byzantine times, it suffered much from the incursions of barbarian peoples, and in the eleventh century it had to be fortified. When the Despotate of Epirus was founded, Ioannina was its capital for a short time, and the town flourished and grew rich. In the fourteenth and fifteenth centuries, a series of foreign princes ruled the town, which in 1430 was handed over as a gift to Sinan Pasha. The townspeople enjoyed extensive privileges until 1611, when they rose - unsuccessfully - in revolt against the Turks. After that time, the Turks settled in the walled castle and the Christian population spread out through the surrounding areas, developing trade and industry. Ioannina attained even greater prosperity under the rule of Ali Pasha (1788-1822). This legendary pasha managed to secure the favour of the Sublime Porte and soon carved out a state of his own, which included parts of what is now Albania. Ioannina also became one of the most important centres of learning of the time, and the court of Ali Pasha

p. 189

Ioannina stands on the shores of Lake Pambotis (length 7.5 km., width 1.5-5 km., average depth 3-4 m.). The Aslan Mosque can be picked out.

was attended by numerous eminent men of letters. But the Sultan resented Ali's successes, and after many years of conspiracy managed to have him beheaded in 1822. The city continued to be important throughout the remainder of the Ottoman period and was finally liberated in 1913.

Ioannina today is a large modern city in which, however, the echoes of the past are easy to hear. Beside the old town, with its quaint old streets, is the **castle**, as it took its final shape under Ali Pasha (1815). Traces of the Byzantine walls have survived in some places. Inside the castle is the **mosque of Aslan Pasha** (1618), which houses the small Historical and Folklore Museum. Nearby are the Turkish **Medresse** or seminary, the **tomb of Aslan Pasha** and the **Turkish Library**. Interesting folklore exhibits are also to be seen in the **Museum of the Society for Epirot Studies**. Ioannina is an important centre for the production of wood-carvings and masterpieces of the art of the local goldsmiths and silversmiths. Examples of their work are on display - and for sale - in the numerous workshops and retail outlets in the town. In the municipal park is an **Archaeological Museum** with fascinating finds from the area around Ioannina: Palaeolithic tools, artefacts from the archaeological site at Dodona and from Ephyra (the Oracle of the Dead on the river Acheron), and other objects dating from between

p. 190
Above: Perama cave.
Centre: view of the village on the island in Lake Pambotis.
Below: gold earring from Epirus (Ioannina Museum).

the Classical and Byzantine periods.

Ioannina takes much of its character from **Lake Pambotis**, the tree-lined banks of which are ideal for romantic strolls, while the waters are much used for practice by rowing teams. The lake is particularly connected with Madame Frosyne, a beautiful lady who was drowned there for having an affair with Ali Pasha's married son Muhtar. In the lake is the idyllic **island of Ioannina**, with an area of some 35 hectares, with reed-banks all around its shores, pretty stone-paved streets, low old-fashioned houses and

boats crowding its harbour with the fish taverns. People were certainly living on the island in the tenth century, but habitation seems to have dated back to prehistoric times. After 1204, the island was the haunt of monks and hermits, who founded some important monastic communities. The monastery of **St Nicholas 'Diliou' or 'Stratigopoulou'** dates from the thirteenth century, and was renovated in the sixteenth century. Its simple, single-aisled main church has marvellous wall-paintings of 1543. The style of these paintings bears resemblances to the ornamentation of the **monastery of St Nicholas 'Philathropinon' or 'Spanou'**, which was built in 1292 and was repaired and extended in the sixteenth century. The wall-paintings of the *katholikon* date from three periods (1531/2, 1542, 1560). The paintings of 1560 were executed by two famous brothers, both priests and both artists of the Epirus School, Yeorgios and Frangos Kontaris, while the paintings in the narthex (1542) have been attributed to Frangos Katelanos of Thebes. Also on the island are the important monasteries of **St John the**

p. 191

The island in Lake Pambotis is quiet, and almost no motor vehicles disturb the peace of its paved alleyways. The little monasteries are enveloped in greenery and kept cool by the nearby waters of the lake. In the background, Ioannina.

Baptist (16th century), of **St Nicholas 'Goumaton'**, also known as **Our Lady of Mercy** from the miraculous icon of the Virgin kept there (15th century), and **St Panteleimon** (17th century). The cells of the St Panteleimon monastery, which are associated with the killing of Ali Pasha, today house the **Museum of the Period before the War of Independence**, whose collection contains documents, ecclesiastical vessels, pieces of jewellery, lithographs, embroidered items, costumes and period weapons.

Four kilometres to the north of Ioannina, near the village of **Perama**, is the cave of the same name - the most impressive horizontal cavern to be seen anywhere in the Balkans. The interior, with its labyrinthine passages, its stalagmites and its stalactites, has yielded the bones and teeth of a species of bear unknown elsewhere in Greece.

p. 192
Bronze ewer from Dodona (Ioannina Museum).

DODONA

Dodona was one of the most ancient and the most sacred sites in Greece. The first human habitation dates back to the third millenium BC, while in the eighteenth century BC the area was occupied by the Elli or Selli, a branch of the Thesprotian tribe. The Selli were dedicated to the service of Zeus, and they it was who founded the Oracle of Dodona, the oldest anywhere in Greece. The predominant cult in the area, before the establishment of Zeus, was that of a pre-Hellenic chthonic deity who survived under the name Dione, wife of Zeus, after the first Greek peoples settled at Dodona.

The pronouncements of the oracle of Dodona were delivered by the Selli, who never washed their feet and slept on the ground so as to draw strength from the earth. There were three ways, all of them connected with sound, in which the oracle could be given. The Selli might interpret the rustling of the leaves of a sacred oak tree next to the temple, or the flight of the doves which lived in the sanctuary. After the eighth century BC, there was a precinct of copper three-legged kettles around the oak tree of Zeus; these touched each other and rang together if one of them was struck. The ringing noises contained the god's message. By the second half of the fourth century BC, only one of the kettles was left, and the people of Corfu dedicated to the sanctuary a bronze statuette of a boy holding a whip. When the wind blew, the whip struck the kettle and so the sounds of the god were still to be heard.

Dodona remained under Thesprotian control until the fifth century BC, when it passed to the Molossians. The **sanctuary of Zeus** originally consisted

of the god's temple (the **'sacred house'**), with its kettles and oak tree, and a building in which the priests lived. In the second half of the fourth century BC, walls were built around the sanctuary and the Sacred House was now inside a precinct. The greatest upsurge in the building activities took place during the reign of King Pyrrhus (297-272 BC): Ionic colonnades were built on three sides of the Sacred House, and the **Ionic temples of Themis and Aphrodite**, the **Doric temple of Heracles**, the **Bouleuterium**, the **Prytaneum** and the monumental **Theatre** of Dodona were constructed. The theatre is still used for performances. In 219 BC, the Aetolian League sacked the sanctuary, but a year later the Koinon of the Epirots defeated the Aetolians in battle and then restored the damaged buildings. At this time, the Sacred House acquired an Ionic porch, making it into a prostyle temple, two Ionic gateways into the theatre were constructed, and the Prytaneum was enlarged with the addition of an entire new complex of buildings. A **Stadium** was built, as the venue for the Naean Games in honour of Zeus Naeus, and so was the **temple of Dione**. Although Dodona passed into Roman hands in 167 BC, the sanctuary continued to operate. In the fourth century AD, an **Early Christian basilica** rose to the west of the temple of Heracles, and the pagan religion was forbidden so that Christianity could flourish. The basilica was reconstructed in the sixth century, in the time of Justinian. In the archaeological site, ruins of all these buildings can be seen, and an oak tree has been planted in more or less the same position in which the sacred tree of Zeus must once have stood.

p. 193

View of the theatre in the sanctuary at Dodona, with a capacity of 17,000. In the background, the snow-covered peaks of Mt Tomaros.

THE ZAGORI VILLAGES - KONITSA - MOLYVDOSKEPASTO

p. 194
Vitsa, a typical Zagori village.

p. 195
The Monastery of Our Lady 'Spiliotissa' stands among steep rocks beside the Vikos gorge below Aristi.

The villages of the **Zagori** area lie in the centre of the Pindus range, between Mt Mitsikeli and the Aoos River. The area was first inhabited in Palaeolithic times, and the ruins of many settlements of the historical period have come to light; then, the whole area was part of the Molossian kingdom. Under Turkish rule, and especially in the eighteenth and nineteenth centuries, the Zagori villages reached a peak of social and economic development, and they were the birthplace of important intellectual figures and benefactors of the Greek nation. Today, there are 46 of the Zagori villages, standing among their green woods and valleys, with their traditional stone-built houses and mansions, their rushing rivers and their numerous fine churches. The east Zagori villages are in a heavily-forested area, while the central villages are those where scheduled settlements are most common. In the centre of the group is the famous **Vikos Gorge**, a national park and a place which will bestow unforgettable memories on visitors, especially those who reach the source of the Voidomatis river. The **Voidomatis**, which is a tributary of the Aoos, runs through the west Zagori villages, which include the picturesque settlement of **Papingo**.

To the north of the Zagori villages is the town of **Konitsa**, on an amphitheatrical site on the verdant slopes

p. 196
Above: bridge over the river Voidomatis in the west Zagori villages.
Below and right: Zagori villages.

of Mt Trapezitsa, close to the impressive Aoos Gorge. Konitsa is the commmercial centre of the area, and it is a traditional place famed throughout Greece for its churches and monasteries. At a distance of 22 km from Konitsa, near the river Sarantaporos, is **Molyvdoskepasto**, a village on the Greek-Albanian border. The area is known for the monastery of the **Dormition of Our Lady**, a foundation dating from the late thirteenth century and ornamented with excellent wall-paintings of the sixteenth century.

ARTA

A rta, chief town of the Prefecture by the same name, stands on the banks of the river Arachthos, on the site of the ancient city of Ambracia which the Corinthians founded in the seventh century BC. Around 295 BC, Ambracia became the capital of the kingdom of Pyrrhus, who built his palace there (the Pyrrheum). The city was deserted after Octavian's victory at Actium in 31 BC, since the inhabitants were forcibly moved to the new

city of Nicopolis. In 1205, Arta became the capital of the Despotate of Epirus, founded by Michael I Angelus Comnenus. During this period, the city flourished, was fortified, and acquired the castle which can still be seen today. Among the structures dating from the time of the Despotate are a number of churches which in artistic terms in no way lag behind those of Mystras and Constantinople itself. They include the churches of **St Theodora** (a three-aisled basilica, c. 1283), built over the tomb of Theodora, consort of Michael Ducas, **St Basil** (a 13th century basilica), and **Our Lady 'Parigoritissa'**, a church whose architecture is unique. It was founded in 1283-1296 by the Comnenus Despots Nicephorus I, his wife Anna, and their son Thomas, all of the Ducas sub-family. Inside the unusual octagonal structure are early pieces of statuary, superb mosaics from the period of the Palaeologi, and more recent wall-paintings.

Close to the town of Arta are a number of equally important churches: the Monastery of **Kato Panayia**, which has

p. 197

Above: the river Voidomatis flows through the stunning Vikos gorge.

Below: the creative effects of erosion, near Papingo in the west Zagori villages.

a *katholikon* in the three-aisled cruci-form-roofed type (mid-13th century), the Monastery of **Our Lady 'Vlacher-na'** (mid-13th century), where the princes of the Comnenus-Ducas family lie buried, and others. Near the famous bridge of Arta is the **church of St Basil**, dating from the second half of the ninth century (in the free cruciform style). The **bridge** of Arta, an Early Christian structure to which additions were made in the thirteenth and sixteenth centuries, was the inspiration for a famous folk song and also for the tragedy by Nikos Kazantzakis entitled *The Chief Mason*.

p. 198
Below: base of a Roman statue from Nicopolis, with a depiction of the Battle of the Amazons in relief. In the early Byzantine period, the Christians erased part of the scene and added a mosaic showing a female and a male figure (above).

The base was used as part of an ambo (Nicopolis Museum).

PREVEZA - NICOPOLIS

Preveza, near the mouth of the Ambracian Gulf, is the chief town of the Prefecture of Preveza. The town was founded by Pyrrhus in 290 BC in honour of his mother-in-law Berenice, wife of Ptolemy of Egypt. In 31 BC, **cape Actium** on the other side of the gulf was the scene of the sea-battle between Mark Antony and Octavian. There is a superb view across the Ambracian Gulf and the scene of the battle from the **Venetian castle** of Preveza. The Venetians took the town in 1499 and held it until forced to surrender to the French in 1797. A year later, Preveza passed into Turkish hands, where it remained until liberation in 1912. Today, Preveza is an attractive port with some very attractive villages and superb beaches in the vicinity.

Seven km. to the north-east of Preveza is the archaeological site of **Nicopolis**, the city founded by Octavian (Augustus) to celebrate his victory at Actium in 31 BC. In the Early Christian period, the **walls** of the city were repaired and extended, and a number of important **basilicas** (6th century AD) were constructed and can still be seen today. Most of these churches were sumptuously built, and ornamented with mosaics and marble tesselation (basilicas A 'Doumetiou', B 'Alkison', C, D, E and F). The archaeological site has a little **museum** with finds from the Roman and Early Christian periods.

EPHYRA
(THE ACHERON ORACLE OF THE DEAD)

To the north of Preveza, close to the ancient city of Ephyra, the ruins have been discovered of the Oracle of the Dead by the river Acheron, which the myths held to be one of the entrances to Hades, the kingdom of the Underworld. Homer's description, in the *Odyssey*, of his hero's descent into the Underworld is in many ways reminiscent of the landscape near Lake Acherusia. The Oracle, which stands on the north-west shores of the lake, was a cave-like sanctuary in which the prophecies were delivered with the help of the souls of the dead. Before questioning the dead, the faithful had to purify themselves and sacrifice, and then took part in ritual banquets. The remains of the Oracle came to light beneath the **Monastery of St John the Baptist**. The sanctuary flourished in the third and second centuries BC, but we know that it was operating as far back as the eighth century BC.

p. 199

Above: the crypt beneath the main hall or the 'dark palace of Hades' at the Oracle of the Dead by the river Acheron.

Below: the Alkison basilica, Nicopolis.

THE IONIAN ISLANDS

p. 200

Above, left: the Caretta-caretta turtle is one of the threatened species still found on Zakynthos.

Above, right: Myrtos beach, Cephalonia.

Below: the central section of the Gorgo pediment from the temple of Artemis on Corfu (585 BC, Corfu Museum).

There are seven Ionian Islands, of which Corfu, Cephalonia, Zakynthos, Lefkada, Ithaca and Paxi are in the Ionian Sea, while Cythera lies off the Peloponnese and belongs administratively to the Prefecture of Piraeus.

Corfu was traditionally taken to be the island of the Phaeacians, the last stop on the wanderings of Odysseus before he reached home after the Trojan Wars. Archaeological investigations have shown that the island was inhabited in Palaeolithic times, and in the historic period it was colonised first by Eretria and then by Corinth (in the 7th century BC). While Corinth still dominated, and later, in the sixth century BC, it flourished and was an important trading post. In 435 BC, the clash between Corfu and its mother city of Corinth was one of the reasons for the outbreak of the Peloponnesian War, during which the island suffered badly from vicious civil strife. After the fourth century BC, Corfu passed through the hands of Sparta, Syracuse, King Pyrrhus of Epirus, Macedon and Illyria, putting itself under Roman protection in 229 BC. During the Roman civil wars of the first century BC, Corfu took the side of Antony and was devastated by the armies of Agrippa for its pains. However, it soon recovered, was rebuilt, and flourished again. Some

◄ *p. 201*
Above: Vlacherna Monastery on Pontikonisi, Corfu.
Below, left: Fiskardo, Cephalonia.
Below, right: Nidri, Lefkada.

p. 202
Views of Corfu
Above:Palaiokastritsa
Below:Assos, Cephalonia.
Centre: view of Corfu town.

interesting remains of ancient Corfu have survived, including the **circular Tomb of Menecrates** (late 7th century BC), traces of the **Temple of Artemis Gorgo** (590-580 BC), the impressive west pediment of which, depicting the myth of the Medusa Gorgo is in Corfu Museum, ancient **houses** on the Kanoni promontory, **sanctuaries of Hera and Apollo** (6th century BC) on the Mon Repos estate, sections of the fifth and fourth century BC **walls**, **baths**, **monuments** and **colonnades** of the Roman period. The impressive **church**

of Sts Jason and Sosipatros, who introduced Christianity to Corfu, dates from around 1000 AD.

Cephalonia is the largest island in the Ionian group and has been inhabited since prehistoric times. In the historical period, four city-states developed on the island, retaining their bonds with Athens down to the time when the Macedonians arrived as conquerors in 218 BC. After 187 BC Cephalonia was part of the Roman Empire, and under Byzantium it was head of an administrative district which took its name.

Lefkada, which some scholars have identified as the Ithaca of Homer, is actually linked to mainland Greece by a bridge. In antiquity, it would have been fairer to describe it as a peninsular offshoot of Acarnania, from which the first Corinthian colonists, of the seventh century BC, isolated it by digging a channel. In the Classical period, Leucas sided with the policies of Corinth, and in 338 BC it was taken by Macedon. In 260 BC it was the centre of the federation of Acarnanian cities, and in 197 BC it became part of Roman territory.

In 31 BC a large part of the population was forced to move to Nicopolis, and the island declined into obscurity.

According to tradition, **Zakynthos** was part of the kingdom ruled by Odysseus. In the historical period, it was dominated by Athens (455 BC) and then ruled by Sparta (430 BC), Macedon and Rome (150 BC). In 1204 it fell to the Franks, and in 1484 to the Venetians.

Ithaca (Ithaki) is known to the world from the exploits of Odysseus, the hero of Homer's epics, whose passion for his homeland took him across the seas and

p. 203

Above: Nidri, Lefkada.

Below: Couloura, Corfu.

to unknown lands before good fortune led him home again. Archaeological excavations have confirmed that the island was inhabited as far back as the third millenium BC. Much light is shed upon all the stages in the history of Ithaca by the finds housed in the archaeological museum at Vathy and by the archaeological sites all over the island.

The history of the tiny island of **Paxi** was bound up with that of its larger neighbour Corfu. In the Middle Ages, it followed the fate of all the Ionian Islands.

Cythera (Kithira), off the south coast of the Peloponnese, was first inhabited in prehistoric times. The finds revealed by excavations at Kastri proved that at this time there was an important Minoan colony, dating from the Late

Palace period (1700-1450 BC). A local tradition relates that the goddess Aphrodite was born on Cythera, thus accounting for her epithet Cytheria. In the historical period, Cythera belonged first to Argos and then to Sparta. The ancient capital of the island has been

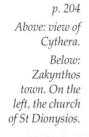

p. 204
Above: view of Cythera.
Below: Zakynthos town. On the left, the church of St Dionysios.

found at Palaiokastro, where traces of its walls may be seen.

To the south-east of Cythera is the little island of **Antikithira**, off the coast of which was found the superb bronze statue of the fourth century BC known as the Kouros of Anticythera.

It was not until the period of Venetian rule that the Ionian islands first formed a single administrative unit. The Venetians took over the islands gradually, between 1386 and 1664, holding them until surrender to the French in 1797, after which they passed to a Russo-Turkish alliance in 1799. In 1800, the Septinsular Republic was formed, under the protection of the Sultan, and in 1807 the Ionian Islands returned to French control. The British extended their power over the area in the period down to 1819, placing all the islands under their protection. Unification with Greece was achieved in 1864.

Today, each of the islands has a character of its own. Yet they are all green and verdant, with superb clean beaches and plenty of sights to see. Cosmopolitan Corfu, with its narrow alleys and tall buildings which bring to mind the cities of Italy, wooded Cephalonia with its high mountains, Lefkada with the Venetian castle of Santa Maura, Zakynthos which the Venetians called 'fiore de Levante', the flower of the east, barren Ithaca, the symbol of ideals and goals, and quiet Paxi: these are true jewels in the crown not only of Greece but of the whole Mediterranean.

p. 205
Nidri, Lefkada.

MACEDONIA

p. 206

Above: detail of the famous Derveni krater (330-320 BC, Vergina Arch. Museum).

Below: Golden head of Hercules, from Derveni (Vergina Arch. Museum).

Macedonia is one of the northern geographical regions of Greece, on its borders with the other Balkan countries. To the south-east, Macedonia is washed by the Aegean Sea, which forms along its coast the Thermaic Gulf, the Gulf of Cassandra, the Gulf of Athos, the Strymonic Gulf and the Gulf of Kavala. To the south, Macedonias borders on Epirus and Thessaly. Between the Thermaic and Strymonic Gulfs is the peninsula of Chalcidice, and further to the east is Thasos, the only island in Macedonia. The soil of Macedonia is particularly fertile, and there are extensive plains (of Thessaloniki, Chalcidice, Serres and Drama) in between the high mountain ranges: Pieria (2198 m.), Vitsi (2128 m.), Vermio (2056 m.), Athos (2033 m.), and others. The acquifer is of particular interest and significance in Macedonia, which is crossed by the major rivers of Greece (the Aliakmon, the Axios, the Strymonas, the Nestos) and contains many of the country's lakes (those of Kastoria, the Large and Small Prespa, Vegoritida, Volvi, Doirani and Kerkinitida).

Macedonia is the part of Greece in which the earliest traces of human habitation have been found. The cave of Petralona has yielded a skull of Neanderthal Man, dating from the Palaeolithic era. Habitation during the Neolithic period has been confirmed on a number of Macedonian sites (Nea Nikomideia, Drama and elsewhere), and the first Greek-speaking tribes seem to have settled in the high Pindus around 2000 BC. During the centuries which

through all the then known world. The epoch of Philip II of Macedon - to use the conventional nomenclature - and his son Alexander brought Macedonia to the peak of its renown and prosperity. After the death of Alexander, Macedonia was the homeland of a great empire divided into the kingdoms of his successors. In 168 BC, the battle of Pydna marked the beginning of Roman control over Macedonia, and of renewed prosperity. After this time, many settlers moved from the west into Macedonian territory, gradually becoming assimilated into the Greek population. When the capital of the Roman Empire moved east to Constantinople in 324 AD, Macedonia as a whole - and Thessaloniki in particular - flourished as hardly ever before. But in the seventh century AD Slavic tribes moved into the area, as a consequence of the creation of a Bulgarian state around a nucleus of Slavs and Finno-Tataric peoples. The Bulgarians tried repeatedly to subjugate Byzantium, but in the end it was their state which was overthrown, by Basil II, 'the Bulgar-slayer', in the eleventh century. After an attack - on a limited scale - by the Serbs in the fourteenth century, Macedonia fell into Turkish hands during the course of the fifteenth century. The struggle for liberation began at the same time as in southern Greece, but it came to an unhappy end. At a time when the rest of Greece was free, Macedonia was still having to deal with the threat of the Bulgarian Exarchate, a menace which became particularly pronounced in 1903-4. The armed 'Macedonian struggle' lasted until 1908, and was ultimately successful in its aims, since Macedonia was finally liberated after the Balkan Wars of 1912-13.

followed, these first Greeks separated into three distinct groups, the most numerous of which was the Macedni. They scattered towards the south, and a subdivision of the tribe, the Macedonians, occupied what is now western and southern Macedonia. The Dorians - as they are called - also split off from the original tribe, extending as far south as the Peloponnese. In the historical period, the Macedonians were at first cut off from the cultural developments of southern Greece, and there was a tendency for them to move into the eastern territories of what is now Macedonia. But we know that they were in touch with the rest of Greece during the seventh century BC, thanks to the colonies which the southern cities had founded in Chalcidice. This southern influence increased still further during the Classical period. The similarities in the sphere of art and the countless inscriptions in Greek found in Macedonia leave no room for doubt that communication between the two parts of the Greek world was never really interrupted. Indeed, it was through the campaigns of Alexander the Great, the Macedonian, that the culture of Greece was disseminated

DION

In antiquity, Dion was the most important shrine of the Macedonians, and one of the most sacred places anywhere in Greece. The city was built, at the foot of Mt Olympus and the Pieria range, in a strategic position no more than one kilometre from the sea (silting has considerably increased the distance today). The site was crossed by the river Baphyras, up which it could be reached from the sea.

Outside the **walls** of Dion, built in the fourth century BC, stood all the **shrines**, the **stadium** and two **theatres**. The most important **sanctuary** was dedicated to **Zeus** and the **Pierian Muses**, and it attracted huge crowds of visitors during the annual festival, called 'the Olympia at Dion'. King Archelaus reorganised the festival in the fifth century BC. Philip II visited the sanctuary before and after the battle of Chaironeia in 338 BC, while four years later Alexander came to sacrifice and pray before setting off on his campaign into Asia. Nearby, also outside the walls, excavations have revealed **sanctuaries of Demeter** (500 BC), of **Asclepius** and of **Dionysus**, together with the ruins of a **composite sanctuary** with three temples dedicated to Artemis and Aphrodite, Isis Tyche and Isis Lochia. In the Early Christian period, a three-aisled **basilica** was built to the north of the sanctuaries, and the remains of it can still

p. 209

The temples of the goddess Isis at Dion (fourth century BC - second century AD).

be seen today. Another Early Christian **basilica** has survived within the city itself.

The ruins of the city of Dion, which was built on the Hippodamian system, have yielded the foundations of many **houses**. Among them is a large complex of buildings which has a superb mosaic floor (showing the epiphany of Dionysus, 200 AD). A **Roman baths building,** a small **Odeum** and sections of the **ancient Agora** have also been excavated, while outside the city a **cemetery** with some Macedonian tombs has been discovered. Dion went into decline and was ultimately abandoned after the fifth century AD.

Today, there is a **museum** close to the archaeological site, with interesting finds which testify to the degree of development Dion once attained.

KASTORIA

Kastoria, chief town of the Prefecture of the same name, stands on the shores of Lake Kastoria and is one of the most important and historic cities of Western Macedonia. The site was first settled in the prehistoric period, as we know from the finds from the **Dispili site**, where an important Neolithic lakeside settlement has been excavated. The first reference to the city by the name Kastoria dates from the sixth century AD, when it began to develop at the outset of a period of considerable prosperity. In the sixth century AD, it was fortified by Justinian, but this did not prevent it falling in 990 to Tsar Samuel of Bulgaria and in 1083 to the Normans. After 1204, it formed part of the Despotate of Epirus,

p. 210-211

Views of the attractive town of Kastoria, on the shores of the lake by the same name.

then passing to the Empire of Nicaea (1251) and to Stepan Dushan of Serbia (14th century). In 1385, the Turks captured the city, and it remained in their hands until liberation in 1912.

Today, Kastoria is known worldwide for the production and marketing of furs, an industry whose beginnings can be traced back to the Byzantine period. The city itself is among the most attractive towns Greece can boast, partly as a result of its idyllic **lake**. The natural beauties of the en-

vironment can be seen in conjunction with the invaluable Byzantine monuments, which have survived in good condition down to the present day. Among these treasures we may note: the small three-aisled basilicas of **St Stephen** (10th century), **Sts Cosmas and Damian** (1000) and the **Archangel of the Cathedral** (10th century); the three-apsed church of **Our Lady 'Koumbelidiki'** (mid-9th century); and the single-aisled churches of **St Nicholas 'Kasnitzis'** (12th century) and **St Athanasius 'Mouzakis'** (14th century). Also of interest is the monastery of **Our Lady 'Mavriotissa'**, on the banks of the lake, 3 km. to the south of Kastoria. The *katholikon* and the chapel of St John preserve superb wall-paintings of the eleventh century. Since 1989, Kastoria has had its own **Byzantine Museum**, which has a collection of icons dating from between the twelfth and the seventeenth centuries. The old mansions of the town, testimony to its wealth in the seventeenth and eighteenth centuries, are also fascinating. In the old-world quarter of Doltso is the **Folklore Museum**, with exhibits from the everyday life of the people of Kastoria and items connected with the fur trade.

THE PRESPES

O n the borders of Greece with Albania and the Former Yugoslav Republic of Macedonia are the Prespes Lakes (Large and Small), which apart from being a place of great natural beauty are also an invaluable wetland. This is a true museum of natural history, with 185 different species of birds and a vastly varied flora. Small Prespa has two islets, called Vidronisi and Ayios Achilleios. On the latter are the remains of a basilica to **St Achilleus**, built in the late tenth century to house the relics of the saint of that name, who was bishop of Larisa in the reign of Constantine the Great. There are many more notable Byzantine monuments throughout the area, and on cliffs of the bay near the village of **Psarades** are wall-paintings showing Our Lady.

p. 212
Views of the Prespes, two lakes of exceptional natural beauty which have 1,500 species of flora and numerous rare birds and animals.

p. 213
View of Edessa.

EDESSA

E dessa is the chief town of the Prefecture of Pella. This attractive modern town is known principally for its impressive **waterfall**, which is very high and conceals a number of caves with stalactites and stalagmites. Edessa was once identified with ancient Aegae, capital of Macedonia, but this view has now been abandoned. Nonetheless, Edessa was one of the important fortresses of Macedonia throughout the region's history. Excavations have brought to light a **wall** dating from the fourth century BC (with Roman and Byzantine additions), and various finds from the surrounding area are on display in the town's **archaeological museum**.

PELLA

It was to Pella, a little town on the shores of the Thermaic Gulf, that the capital of Macedon was moved from Aegae when Archelaus was king in about 400 BC. We know from written records that Archelaus built a sumptuous palace there, which he had decorated with wall-paintings by the renowned artist Zeuxis. Archelaus' court was a magnet for personalities in the world of the arts and letters of the day. They included the great Euripides, who ended his days in Pella. Excavations have brought to light sections of a **palace**, most of which can be dated to the time of Philip II. While Philip was king of Macedon, Pella flourished, and expanded beyond what had once been its city limits. The town, arranged on the Hippodamian system of urban planning, was surrounded by a **wall**. The earliest traces of this fortification date, once again, from the time of Philip II, but most of the circuit was constructed under Cassander, in whose reign (350-297 BC) Pella flourished once again.

At the northernmost edge of the city is the **acropolis**, with the royal palace. In the centre was the **Agora**, the ruins of whose buildings date from the Hellenistic period.

The Agora of Pella consists of an open **plaza** surrounded by **colonnades**, used for commercial purposes. To the south of the Agora, archaeologists have uncovered three building zones with **administrative** and **religious buildings** (north zone) and **private residences** (two southern zones). Two of the

p. 214
The archaeological site at Pella.

houses were ornamented with mosaics of incalculable artistic value (the 'House of the Rape of Helen' and the 'House of Dionysus' 330-300 BC).

Pella was a centre for the cult of the wine-god Dionysus, partly because the area produced the 'grapes of Pella' so famous in antiquity. Athena, too, was worshipped in her warlike capacity (Athena Alcidemus), as was Heracles, who was believed to have been the primogenitor of the royal dynasty of Macedon. To the north of the Agora, archaeologists have discovered a group of religious buildings dedicated to the shared cult of **Cybele** and **Aphrodite**, and to the north-east, outside the walls, is a sanctuary of Demeter and Kore (the **Thesmophorium**). Another sanctuary, in the form of a *tholos* and dedicated to a cult hero, has been found to the south

west of the site, and to the east of the Agora is a **cemetery** with burials dating from the period from the fourth century BC to the Hellenistic period. One very interesting find is what has been called the **Phacus**, a mound of earth three kilometres south of Pella consisting of the detritus of uninterrupted human habitation of the site. The Macedonian kings walled the Phacus and used it as a treasury, linking it by a bridge to the main gate of the city.

Close to the archaeological site is a **museum** with finds from the city and its environs. The finds show that Pella had been inhabited since the prehistoric period and was a highly-developed city long before it became the capital of the Macedonians. The most important exhibits are, of course, those dating from after 400 BC.

p. 215
Mosaic floor from the archaeological site at Pella, fourth century BC.

NAOUSA - LEFKADIA

The large and attractive town of **Naousa,** in the Prefecture of Imathia, stands in the vicinity of ancient Mieza. The modern town was founded during the period of Ottoman rule, when it succeeded in winning significant privileges from the conquerors and in developing into an important centre for trade, industry and the arts and letters. The people of Naousa were successful for many years in fighting off Ali Pasha, to whose power they eventually succumbed in 1804. The town was looted by the Turks in 1822. Naousa was rebuilt in the mid-nineteenth century and liberated, to be incorporated into modern Greece, in 1912.

Not far from Naousa is the village of **Lefkadia**, where four superb Macedonian tombs have been discovered. **Macedonian tombs** were vaulted, underground, stone-built structures consisting of one, or perhaps two, chambers in which the aristocratic dead of the Macedonian families were interred. The tombs are monumental buildings in which particular care was taken over the facade: this was constructed so as to resemble a temple, with features from both the Doric and the Ionic orders. Inside, the walls were usually painted with plant motifs, or with figurative scenes. The most impressive of the Lefkadia tombs is that called the **'Tomb of the Judgement'**, which has two chambers and a double facade leading up to a pediment ornamented with important art-works. The other tombs are the **Kinch** tomb, the **Lyson and Callicles** tomb, and the **'tomb of the rosettes'**.

p. 216
View of
Naousa

VERRIA (BERROEA) -
NEA NIKOMEDIA

Verria is the chief town of the Prefecture of Imathia. It stands among the lower foothills of Mt Vermion, near the plain crossed by the river Tripotamos. The fall of this river and the power it produced made possible the industrial development of Verria, which is nonetheless a picturesque town with a traditional architectural physiognomy all its own.

Human beings have inhabited the area around Verria since the sixth millennium BC, at the latest. Near the town, archaeologists have excavated the Neolithic settlement of **Nea Nikomedia**, which consists of houses built of beams, tree branches and mud. The finds from Nea Nikomedia are on display in **Verria Museum**, which also has important exhibits relating to the history of the town. The earliest inhabitants of Verria were Bryges from Thrace, who, however, were soon displaced by Macedonians. Archaeologists have also unearthed evidence of the history of Verria dating

back to the fourth century BC (the **cemetery**, the **stadium** and the **agora** of the ancient city).

In the period of Roman rule, which began in 168 BC, the area flourished, and after the early eleventh century it was a separate administrative region of Macedonia. There is testimony to the prosperity of Verria in Byzantine times to be seen in the 48 churches which have survived down to the present day. Of particular interest are the **Old Cathedral** (1070-1080), whose wall-paintings were executed over the period between the twelfth and fourteenth centuries, the church of the **Resurrection of Christ** (1315), whose wall-paintings are the work of the famous fourteenth-century artist Yeorgios Callergis, and the numerous churches dating from the period of Turkish control (1387-1912)

*p. 217
Below:
traditional house
in Veria.*

VERGINA

p. 218
*Above: gold panel with battle scenes from
the quiver accompanying the burial in the
Great Tumulus at Vergina (Vergina
Archaeological Museum).*

*Below: ivory head from Vergina, probably
depicting Philip II.*

p. 219
*The silver pitcher from the Tomb of the
Prince (Vergina Archaeological Museum).*

Vergina is the most important archaeological site of Macedonia; after a century of excavations by Hammond and Andronikos, it was finally identified as Aegae, the old capital of the Macedonian kingdom. The site was occupied, without interruption, from 1000 BC into the Roman period. The earliest finds on the site come from what is called the **cemetery of the tombs**, which came to light between the villages of Vergina and Palatitsia. The first burials were carried out between 1000 and 700 BC, and they are testimony to the existence at this date of a large settlement of an advanced economic and cultural level which had systematic contact with the more southerly parts of Greece.

The second phase of tomb-building took place in the fourth and third centuries BC. On the west edge of the cemetery is the **Great Tumulus**, a tomb of unusual size measuring 110 metres in diameter and 12 metres in height. This is one of the most important archaeological discoveries of all time. In the earth mound of the tumulus itself, the archaeologists found scattered fragments of funerary *stelae* (Vergina Museum), dating from the late fourth and early third century BC, with Greek names - thus serving as evidence of the Greekness of Macedonia at this early date. Further digging revealed that the tumulus contained the sumptuous tombs of the Macedonian kings. The Great Tumulus contained two Macedonian

tombs which had escaped the attention of the grave-robbers, a shaft burial, and a monument to the fallen. The shaft tomb, known as the **Persephone tomb**, has an interior decorated with a superb painting on the theme of the Rape of Persephone by Pluto (340 BC). One of the Macedonian tombs, called the **Tomb of the Prince**, had two chambers with a monumental facade, and it contained the bones of a young man - interred about 325 BC - accompanied by very rich funerary offerings. The other is the most important of all since it has been identified as the **tomb of King Philip II of Macedon**. After the assassination of Philip in 336 BC, his son Alexander - the Great - was proclaimed king, and his first concern was to inter his father. As a result, the chamber was built rather hurriedly; the corpse was cremated outside it, and an antechamber was then constructed. It was not until some time later that the facade was completed: it had to be monumental enough for the tomb of a king. The facade is in the form of a Doric temple, on the frieze of which is a striking painted scene showing a hunt in a forest. The figures of Philip and Alexander have been recognised among those depicted. The precious offerings left with the occupant of the tomb - Vergina Museum - date from between 350 and 310 BC, thus leaving scarcely any doubt that this was the tomb of Philip II. Close to the tomb was found a **monument to the fallen**, which is believed to have been used as part of the cult of Philip, who was worshipped as a hero after his death.

A total of eleven Macedonian tombs have come to light in the vicinity of Vergina, all of them yielding finds of the greatest value. Of course, the sites of the **palace** of Vergina and of the the-

atre in which Philip was assassinated are also fascinating. The palace, which has verandas on three of its sides, consisted of a large number of rooms arranged around a large peristyle courtyard. The royal apartments on the south side had three rooms with mosaic floors, and one of the explanations of the circular room discovered on the east side of the monumental entrance is that it was the throne room. The palace of Vergina, constructed in the late fourth or early third century, was used by the Macedonian kings even when their capital had moved to Pella, as it did in 400 BC. It was the custom, apart from anything else, to bury dead kings at Aegae and to celebrate there the important events in their lives. One of those events proved to be the reason for the assassination of Philip II. During the wedding of his daughter Cleopatra, in 336 BC, the king made a triumphal entry into the **theatre** of Vergina - from its east side - and it was there that he was attacked by the murderer, whose name was Pausanias. The theatre has been excavated, to the north of the palace, and it stands there today as a mute witness to the events of 336 BC.

Further to the north, beyond the theatre, is a **temple dedicated to Eucleia,** a Macedonian deity cognate with Aphrodite. Close to the temple, the archaeologists found an inscription on a votive offering mentioning Euridice daughter of Sirra, mother of Philip II, as its donor. This inscription, dating from the second half of the fourth century BC and providing yet another link to the Macedonian royal family, is one more confirmation that Vergina is ancient Aegae.

p. 221
Gold larnax from Vergina ornamented with the Macedonian symbol of the sixteen-pointed star. It probably contained the bones of Philip II (Vergina Archaeological Museum).

THESSALONIKI

p. 222

Above: details of the wall-paintings in the church of St Demetrius.

Below: gold wreath from Vergina (Vergina Archaeological Museum).

p. 223

The White Tower, emblem of the modern city of Thessaloniki.

Thessaloniki, at the head of the Thermaic Gulf, is the chief town of the Prefecture of the same name, and is also the second-largest city in Greece and its most important harbour after Piraeus. Yet Thessaloniki has no cause to feel itself inferior to Athens: it is an attractive city, with a long cultural tradition, with a busy artistic and cultural scene, with highly-developed industrial and commercial sectors, and with a bustling port. It is also the administrative and communications centre of the whole of northern Greece.

Prehistory - Classical Times

The history of the area around Thessaloniki dates back whole millennia. The first human beings seem to have settled there in Neolithic times, and habitation has been continuous down to the present day. Long before Thessaloniki was founded, there was a city on the same site called **Therme**, which gave its name to the Thermaic Gulf. Although its exact position has not been determined, its existence is known from ancient sources dating as far back as the fifth century BC. The need for communication with other Greek cities led Cassander, king of Macedon, to unify the twenty five little towns along the Thermaic Gulf, and in 316/315 BC to found a new city to which he gave the name of his wife, sister of Alexander the Great: Thessaloniki. Be-

p. 224

Above: Diikitiriou
Square,
Thessaloniki.

Below: view of the
city and part of its
Byzantine walls.

fore long, the new city - built on the Hippodamian system - had been surrounded by walls and had developed into an important centre for trade and shipping. Very little has remained of this stage in its history, but we know from historical sources that it had a sumptuous palace, an Agora, a gymnasium and many sanctuaries. A **sanctuary of the Egyptian god Sarapis**, dating from the third century BC, has come to light, together with some **Macedonian tombs** and extensive Hellenistic **cemeteries**.

The Roman Period

In 168 BC Thessaloniki was taken by the Romans, and in 146 BC it was made capital of the province of Macedonia. In 42 BC, it was declared a free city, with a democratic system of government, the right to elect its own rulers and issue its own coinage. In the Augustan period, it flourished and was particularly prominent in the arts, retaining its Greek physiognomy and resisting Roman penetration. Down to the first years of the Christian era it

was a cultural centre which was the resort of many figures in the arts and letters, and it attracted numerous immigrants. Those were the circumstances in which the Jewish community of Thessaloniki first developed. In 49 AD, the Jews and pagans of Thessaloniki heard the Christian gospel preached by the Apostle Paul, and the nucleus of a Christian community began to form.

Many important monuments of the Roman period have survived in Thessaloniki, and give a good idea of the city's development at that time. The **Roman Forum** dates from the second century BC, the period of Antoninus and Severus; it consists of two adjacent squares with colonnades housing shops and administrative premises. To the east of the north square, an **Odeum** of 293-305 AD has been excavated. However, the most important Roman monument is the **palace of Caesar Galerius Maximianus**, who in 297 AD chose Thessaloniki as his seat of government. The palace is a complex of buildings constructed in

p. 225
Thessaloniki seen from the Thermaic Gulf.

305, consisting of the Rotunda, the Arch, the main palace, the Octagon and the Hippodrome. The **Rotunda** is the building furthest to the north, and it was inten-ded either as a temple or as the Mausoleum of Galerius himself. Its design is influenced by that of the Pantheon in Rome, being circular in plan and roofed with a dome which has an aperture in the centre. In the mid-fifth century, the Rotunda was converted into a Christian church dedicated to **St George**, and it was ornamented with important mosaics of which some fragments have survived. To the south of the Rotunda is the triumphal arch of Galerius, called the **Camara**, which was erected to commemorate his victories over the Persians in 296-297 AD. The pillars supporting the arches of the monument are ornamented with reliefs showing battles against the Persians. A street led through the Camara to the **palace proper**, a luxurious building with rooms arranged around a central courtyard with a colonnade. To the east was the **Hippodrome**, and to the south was the **Octagon**, which may well have served as the throne-room. Excavations have also brought to light a large number of Roman **baths**, together with traces of the **Via Regia**, which was an extension of the Via Egnatia.

Byzantine Period

It was in the Byzantine period that Thessaloniki flourished as never before, and became the most important political and economic centre of Macedonia, as well as being the focus of Christianity there. The Byzantine emperors took an interest in the city from an early date, beginning with Constantine the Great himself, who reconstructed the harbour. In the late fourth and early fifth century, strong new walls were built, and sections of them have survived down to the present day. Sometime during the fifth century, the churches of St Demetrius, of the Acheiropoietos and of the Blessed David (Latomou Monastery) were founded. The **basilica of St Demetrius** was constructed on a site previously occupied by Roman baths, directly on the spot where the saint is traditionally supposed to have been martyred in 303 AD. The church of St Demetrius is one of the most important monuments of Christian art of any period, in terms both of its architecture and of its ornamentation with sculptures and marbles. Inside the five-aisled basilica are eleven mosaics created between the fifth and the ninth centuries, most of them showing the saint whose name the church commemorates. The church of the **Acheiropoietos** is a three-aisled basilica with mosaics of the fifth century AD and wall-paintings of the thirteenth.

The dome of the cruciform church of the **Blessed David** preserves an even more important mosaic composition created in the late fifth century.

Yet another interesting mosaic is to be seen in the church of the **Holy Wisdom** ('Ayia Sofia'), which was constructed in the seventh century on a site previously occupied by a fifth-century basilica with five aisles. The new church, whose exterior is solid and almost for bidding, is in the domed basilica type. Its interior has important mosaics and wall-paintings created between the eighth and twelfth centuries.

In the period between the sixth and the eleventh centuries, Thessaloniki suffered much from the incursions of Slavs, Arabs, Saracen pirates and Bulgars. In 995, Tsar Samuel of Bulgaria succeeded in overcoming

p. 226

Above: the basilica of St Demetrius, fifth century.

Midle:the church of the Holy Wisdom, seventh century.

Below: part of the Byzantine walls of Thessaloniki.

p. 227

The 'Rotunda' (church of St George), Thessaloniki.

p. 228

Left: the basilica of St Nicholas 'Orphanos' in the Upper City.

Right: the church of the Prophet Elijah is of the triconch type, one of the most complex Byzantine forms.

p. 229

Left: detail of the wall-paintings in one of the city's Byzantine churches.

Right: the church of the Holy Apostles, of the Palaeologan period.

Below: part of Vlatadon Monastery (1360-1370).

the Byzantine army and in occupying the city, which came back into the hands of Byzantium after the victories of the Emperor Basil the Bulgar-Slayer (1014-1019). For some decades there was peace and good order, with development in all possible areas. It was during this time that the **church of Our Lady 'Chalkeon'** was built (1028): in the domed cross-in-square structure, we can see a combination of the architectural trends current in southern Greece with those of Constantinople. The twelfth century was the time of Norman incursions, building up to the occupation of Thessaloniki by Boniface of Monferrat in 1204 and by the Despo-tate of Epirus in 1223. For one more time, the city came back to the Byzantines in 1261, and under the Palaeologus emperors flourished as rarely before and was largely rebuilt. The churches of the **Holy Apostles** (1310-1314, cross-in-square), of **St Catherine** (13th or 14th century, cross-in-square), of **St Panteleimon** (1300-1310, cross-in-square), and of **St Nicholas 'Orphanos'** (early 14th century, three-aisled basilica),

the **chapel of St Euthymius** in the church of St Demetrius (early 14th century, cross-in-square), and **Vlatadon Monastery** (1360-1370, cross-in-square) all date from this time. Most of the churches listed above have wonderful wall-paintings.

Ottoman Times- The Modern Era

After seven years under Venetian rule, Thessaloniki was taken by the Turks in 1430. In 1821, the city rose in support of the War of Independence, and in 1903-1904 it was the operations centre for the Macedonian Struggle. Liberation from the Ottoman Empire finally came in 1912. The year 1917 saw the destruction of much of the city in a catastrophic fire, after which reconstruction followed. Today, apart from the Byzantine treasures mentioned above, there are abundant monuments from the Turkish period to be seen in Thessaloniki. They include the **Hamsa Bey and Alatza Imaret mosques**, quite a number of Turkish baths, and the **Bezesteni**,

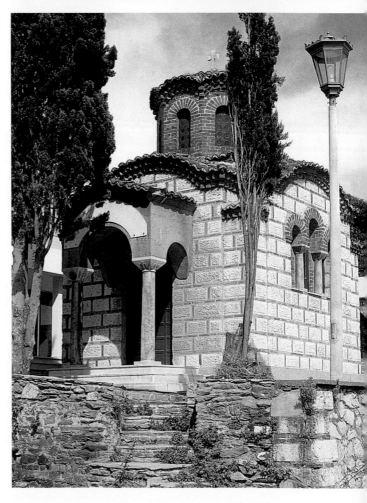

once a shop selling luxury textiles and still in commercial use today.

The modern city stands between the Thermaic Gulf and Mt Hortiatis, and its crown is the picturesque quarter called the **Upper Town**. Up in the Old Town sections of the **walls** - dating back to the original structure of the fourth century AD and including subsequent repairs and extensions - have survived in good condition. The walls of Thessaloniki surrounded the city as far as the seafront, and all along them were towers and bastions. The most notable of these works of fortification was the **White Tower**, built in 1430, in the reign of Murat II, on the site of a Byzantine tower. Today, the tower houses a collection of items from Byzantine and Ottoman times.

MUSEUMS

The most important collection of Byzantine artefacts to be seen in Thessaloniki is in the **Byzantine Museum** of the city, which opened recently and is an example of the most up-to-date concepts of museum theory. Its collection includes items from the very first years of Christianity, members from Early Christian churches, finds from cemeteries and in connection with the arts of fortification and house-building, coins, lead seals, inscriptions and miniature manuscripts of the Middle Byzantine period, some superb glazed vases of the time of the Palaeologus emperors, the D. Economopoulos collection, the D. Papastratou collection of icons printed on paper, and a tremendous amount of information about the excavations which produced the exhibits, their restoration and the manner in which they have been put on display.

The **Archaeological Museum** of Thessaloniki contains one of the finest collections of antiquities to be seen anywhere in the country. It was set up immediately after the liberation of Thessaloniki, and new finds have been added to it, without interruption, ever since then. In the **vestibule** (Room 3) are the architectural members of an Ionian temple, found scattered all across the city and dating from the late Archaic period. **Rooms 4 and 5** contain sculptures from various sites in Macedonia, dating from between the Archaic and Roman periods.

Room 6, called 'Thessaloniki', gives a clear picture of the history of the city since the Neolithic era. Exhibits from the Roman period, most of them sculptural, are to be seen in **Rooms 7 and 8.**

The prehistoric collection of the Museum, consisting of finds from Central and Western Macedonia, is to be seen in **Room 10,** while **Room 11** contains finds from the Archaic period in Macedonia.

Room 1, which we now enter, houses the artefacts - of the greatest historical interest and, of course, priceless value - from the excavations at Sindos. The exhibits were found in a total of 121 tombs dating from Archaic and early Classical times. In **Room 2** is a reconstruction of the facade of the Macedonian tomb at Ayia Paraskevi, near Thessaloniki, with its marble door, together with the painted marble couch and door from the Macedonian tomb found at Potidaia in Chalcidice.

Fascinating collections of finds are also to be seen in the **Folklore and Ethnological Museum**, the **Museum of the Macedonian Struggle**, and the **National Gallery** (in the building of the State Theatre of Northern Greece). Another of the features for which Thessaloniki is famous world-wide is its **International Trade Fair**, which has been held every September in the city since 1925. Those who visit it will have a chance to see the latest international developments in the worlds of technology, production, commerce and services. Since 1960, the Trade Fair events have included a Festival of Greek Cinema, and since 1961 the Greek Song Festival. The intellectual life of Thessaloniki is particularly lively, partly as a result of the work done by the Aristotle University of Thessaloniki, one of the most important learned institutions in Greece.

THE PETRALONA CAVE

In 1959, the cave called Kokkines Petres ('red stones') at Petralona in Chalcidice was explored for the first time. Apart from its interest for geologists, it also yielded palaeontological finds of the greatest importance, including a skull of Neanderthal Man dating, according to most scholars, from a period some 270,000-240,000 years ago. The skull, of a woman aged approximately 25, is now in the keeping of Thessaloniki University.

p. 230
The strapwork krater from Derveni, showing Dionysus and Ariadne (330-320 BC, Thessaloniki Arch. Museum).

p. 231
The Petralona cave, with its amazing stalactites and stalagmites.

MOUNT ATHOS
(THE HOLY MOUNTAIN)

A thos is the most easterly of the three promontories in which the peninsula of Chalcidice ends. Thanks to its unique monastic community, which has existed on the mountain since the tenth century, Athos is one of the most important places not only in Greece but throughout the Balkans. The 'Holy Mountain', as it is called in Greek, is a self-governing part of Greek territory, where the echoes of the Byzantine past are loud. It is a living museum of Byzantine art, in terms both of the architecture of the monasteries themselves and of the priceless works of art which are jealously guarded within them.

Athos is linked to the rest of Chalcidice by a narrow strip of land only two kilometres in width. Here the historical memories go back to the time of the Persian wars. As the ancient sources themselves tell us, in 480 BC King Xerxes of Persia ordered a channel to be dug across the neck of the promontory, so that his ships would not have to round the stormy cape of Athos on their way south. The traces of **Xerxes' canal** can still be seen today. The remains of ancient monuments have been found throughout the area, testimony to its habitation right down the course of Greek history.

We do not know exactly when Christianity reached Mt Athos, but the traditional account insists that Our Lady herself visited the promontory and preached the new religion. For that reason, it is still forbidden even today for

p. 233

Dionysiou Monastery on Mt Athos stands on a clifftop 80 metres above the sea.

women to tread the soil of Mt Athos. Hermits would seem to have been in the area during the eighth century, and in 961-963, St Athanasius of Athos, a counsellor to Nicephorus Phocas, founded the first monastery, that of Megiste Lavra. After that time, many monks received the support of the emperors of Byzantium in setting up new foundations, the number of which had reached 180 by the thirteenth century. The manner in which the monasteries are governed is still determined by regulations first devised in 973 and replaced in 1393 by a new set on the initiative of Manuel II Palaeologus. Under Ottoman rule, Mt Athos received preferential treatment, and it continued to be the centre of the Orthodox faith, keeping open its schools for monks. The Athonias School, the most famous of these, was established in 1749, and the famous scholar and clergyman Evyenios Voulgaris was appointed to its staff in 1753. Liberation from the Turks came in 1912, and the Holy Mountain was brought under the administrative supervision of the Greek State, though it remains within the spiritual jurisdiction of the Ecumenical Patriarchate in Constantinople.

There are six different types of monastic foundation on Mt Athos: the monasteries themselves, the *sketes*, the *kellia*, the *kalyves*, the *kathismata* and the *hesychasteria*, all of different sizes and functions but all centring on **Karyes**, the only town on the Holy Mountain - a place with some traces of a secular appearance. Today, there are 20 monasteries on the mountain, 17 of them Greek: **St Panteleimon** is Russian, **Chelandarion** is Serbian and **Zographou** is Bulgarian. As we have noted, **Megiste Lavra** was founded in 963 by St Athanasius of Athos. After various

additions, its *katholikon* (1002) took the final Athonite three-apsed form. Basically, this is a cross-in-square structure which apart from its east apse has two additional recesses (the *choroi*) to the north and south, making a total of three. The Athonite type of church soon spread throughout the Balkans, where it was predominant in the Middle Byzantine period. The monastery has some superb wall-paintings, the work of Theophanes of Crete (1535) and Frangos Katelanos (1560), the latter of whom was a representative of the Epirus school of painting.

Vatopaidi Monastery was founded in the tenth century and ornamented with donations from Andronicus Palaeologus and John Cantacuzene,

who is said to have lived there as 'the monk Ioasaph'. The wonderful paintings on the walls of the *katholikon* are among the oldest anywhere on Athos, and some of them date from the eleventh century. The sacristy and the library of the monastery have many treasures.

Iviron Monastery was founded in 979 and its interior preserves wall-paintings of the Cretan School dating from 1572. It also has a fine collection of manuscripts and ecclesiastical artefacts. Wall-paintings of the Cretan School, executed in the sixteenth century, are also to be seen in the monasteries of **Docheiareiou** (11th century), **Koutloumousiou** (13th century) and **St Paul** (10th century), while works

by the Cretan painter Zorzis adorn **Dionysiou Monastery** (14th century). The latter monastery also preserves five icons of the Great Deisis (Intercession) painted in 1542 by Euphrosynos the priest. The painter Theophanes of Crete, whose work we have seen in Megiste Lavra Monastery, is also preserved elsewhere: in **Pantocrator Monastery**, founded in the fourteenth century, in **Stavronikita Monastery**, already in existence in the tenth century, and in the **Protato** (icons).

The Protato is in Karyes, and its church was probably built in the tenth century. The wall-paintings are the work of the painter Manouil Panselinos, and they are fine examples of the style of the thirteenth century (they date from around 1300).

Another trend in the history of wall-painting is to be seen in the *katholikon* of **Xenophontos Monastery** (10th century): it has works painted by the artist Antonios (1544), who continued the anti-classical tradition of the period of the Palaeologus emperors. The remaining monasteries of the Holy Mountain are of no less interest in terms of their art-works and holy relics: they are **Xeropotamou** (10th century), **Karakallou** (11th century), **Philotheou** (10th century), **Simonopetra** (14th century), **Grigoriou** (14th century), **Esphigmenou** (11th century), **Kastamonitou** (before the 14th century), **Chelandarion** (12th century), St **Pantaleimon** (11th century) and **Zographou** (13th century).

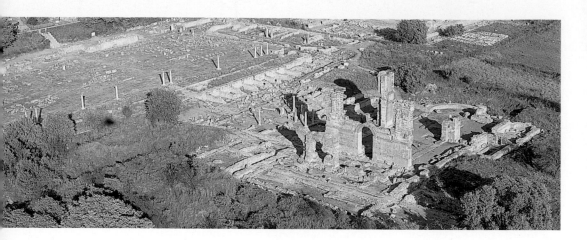

PHILIPPI

p. 238

The archaeological site at Philippi.

p. 239

Basilica B at Philippi, a three-aisled church originally roofed with a complex system of domes; sixth century.

Philippi is 17 km. to the north west of Kavala, between Mt Pangaion and Mt Orvilos. The city was founded by settlers from the island of Thasos in 360/359 BC, and was originally called Crenidae. The new city stood close to the gold and silver mines on Mts Pangaion and Orvilos, in a fertile location which was also a crossroads on the main roads into and through Thrace. Four years after the foundation of Crenidae, the Thasians were compelled to plead with Philip II for his help in beating off the Thracian tribes who lived in their vicinity, and Philip seized the opportunity to become master of the city and rename it Philippi, after himself. In 168 BC, Philippi was taken by the Romans, and in 42 BC it was the site of the battle between Cassius and Brutus, on one side, and Octavian (Augustus) on the other. As a result of Augustus' victory, Roman colonists settled in the area, and a new and important city developed. In 49 AD, St Paul visited Philippi and preached Christianity there. The Christian city flourished for many years, but began to decline after the ninth century AD.

The ruins of Philippi today are testimony to the wealth of the city in the Roman era. All the buildings are enclosed within a strong **wall**, originally constructed in the time of Philip II and rebuilt in the tenth century AD. The **Via Egnatia** passed through the fortified city, and its paving-stones can still be seen. The most important buildings of the city lined the Via Egnatia.

To the north of the site is the **theatre**, dating from the

time of Philip II, together with a **sanctuary of the Egyptian deities** of the second century BC and some smaller **open-air sanctuaries**. On the south side, traces of the **Roman forum** (2nd century BC) have come to light: it contained **workshops, storerooms, adm-nistrative offices,** the **rostrum** from which speakers addressed the public, **fountains** and **colonnades,** a **library** and two small temples, dedicated to **the Emperor Antoninus Pius** and his consort **Faustina**. Still further to the south were another **commercial forum**, a **palaestra** of the second century BC, and Roman **baths**. In the centre of the city, a **Macedonian tomb** of the third century BC has been excavated; above it was a monument at which the memory of the dead hero was honoured. In the fourth century AD, the tomb and its monument were incorporated into the structure of a Christian house of prayer.

The Christian monuments of Philippi are just as important as their Roman predecessors. To date, archaeologists have discovered four **Early Christian basilicas**, of which Basilica B, dating from the sixth century AD, is the most important. Also of great interest is the **Octagon** of Philippi, a church with an octagonal floor plan first constructed in the late fourth century and rebuilt in the fifth and sixth centuries. Some scholars believe this to have been the cathedral church of the city.

Close to the archaeological site, at the spot called **Lydia**, is a stream in which - according to tradition - St Paul baptised a certain Lydia, who was the first Christian convert on European soil. A small church stands on the spot today, to mark the event.

AMPHIPOLIS

The site of Amphipolis is between the mountains of Kerdylio and Pangaio, close to the river Strymon. The area was inhabited in Neolithic times, and later bore the name Ennea Hodhoi, 'nine roads'. Until the fifth century BC, it belonged to the Thracian tribe called the Edonians, who often had to beat off Athenian attempts to conquer them. In 437 BC, Ennea Hodhoi eventually fell to Athens and became an important colony, called Amphipolis. Before taking the city itself, Athens had first seized Eion, the port of Amphipolis, five kilometres to the south at the estuary of the river Strymon, on the gulf of the same name. Eion remained in Athenian hands even when Amphipolis fell to the Spartans, under their general Brasidas, during the Peloponnesian War. Both Brasidas and the Athenian general Cleon were killed at Amphipolis in 422 BC, during one of the most dramatic episodes in the War. From 421 BC to 357 BC, in the time of Philip II, the city remained independent, though under Macedonian suzerainty. In 334 BC, it was from Amphipolis that Alexander the Great set out on his campaign into Asia, with his fleet anchored along the shores of the Strymonic Gulf as far as Eion. The Romans took Amphipolis in 168 BC, and Aemilius Paulus made it the chief town of one of the four sub-provinces into which Macedonia was divided. In the first century BC Amphipolis was devastated by Thracian tribes, and had to be reconstructed by Octavian. In 49 AD the inhabitants of Amphipolis received the gospel, preached by St Paul. The city went into decline after the sixth century AD and references to it cease after the eighth and ninth century, when it suffered from the incursions of the Slavs.

The Classical city of Amphipolis was surrounded by a double wall with a circumference of 7.5 km.

At various periods, the wall was fitted with large numbers of drains which led off the rain water from the inner part of the city to the outside. This was an unusually advanced construction project for its time, and served the purpose of preventing floods which might have damaged the fortifications. To the north-west of the city, very close to the wall, archaeologists have recently discovered a unique find which bears out the description of the Peloponnesian War recorded by the historian Thucydides: this is the famous **bridge over the river Strymon**, the substructure of which - wooden piles and all - was found to have survived intact down the centuries. This was the bridge over which Brasidas passed on his way to the conquest of Amphipolis, and as an archaeological find it is unique in Greece.

Excavations in Amphipolis have brought to light a large number of **private houses** dating from between the fourth century BC and the Hellenistic period. Among the few public buildings to have come to light are a **gymnasium** and auxiliary structures used as far back as the fourth century BC, the remains of a **theatre**, a small **temple of Demeter** from the old city of Ennea Odhoi, a **sanctuary of the Phrygian deities** and a **sanctuary**

dedicated to the Muse Cleio. Among the funerary monuments, three **Macedonian tombs** and the famous **Lion of Amphipolis** stand out. According to the most likely interpretation, the Lion - now restored - crowned a funerary monument in which was the tomb of one of the generals of Alexander the Great, who died in the late fourth century BC after Alexander's campaign in Asia.

Very few traces of Roman Amphipolis have survived: certainly not enough to allow us to reconstruct the city. On the other hand, many monuments from the Early Christian period, when the city was called Chrysoupolis, have been excavated. Four three-aisled **Early Christian basilicas** have been discovered, ornamented with mosaic floors, together with a **hexagonal sacred building** of the sixth century AD.

p. 241
View of Amphipolis

KAVALA

K avala, one of the most attractive towns in Greece, is the chief town of the Prefecture by the same name. The area was colonised by Athens in the fifth century BC and originally named Neapolis. It continued to be an ally of Athens down to the time when it fell to Philip II in the mid-fourth century BC. After that time, it was the port for nearby Philippi, and flourished until the collapse of the Macedonian kingdom itself. In 49 AD, St Paul visited the city, and spread the Christian faith among the local people. The Roman Emperors showed an interest in the development of the city, but in 396 AD it was ravaged by the Goths. In the fifth century AD it was rebuilt, and took the name Christoupolis. Under Byzantium, it was prosperous once more, and fortifications were built. In 1380, the Turks took the city and confined the population within the bounds of the Byzantine castle. Under the Balkan Wars, Kavala - as it had been called since Turkish times - was briefly under Bulgarian occupation before being finally liberated in 1913.

Today, Kavala is a modern city, but it has lost little of the atmosphere of an earlier era. The site of the city is a natural amphitheatre, crowned by the Byzantine **castle** and with a most attractive harbour at its feet. The port of Kavala is the most important centre for the exporting of tobacco from northern Greece, and the city itself has the oldest tobacco processing factories in the area. Among

p. 242

View of Kavala with the old aqueduct and a boatyard where wooden fishing-craft were made.

p. 243

The aqueduct, built by Suleyman the Magnificent, separates the new town from the old quarter. Kavala, on its naturally amphitheatrical site on Mt Symvolo, is a harmonious blend of the traditional and the contemporary.

the sites to be visited in Kavala are the old **aqueduct** (known as the 'Kamares'), dating from the sixteenth century and built by Suleyman the Magnificent, the **house of Mohamet Ali** (1804-1848), the governor of Egypt, who was born in Kavala, large numbers of **Byzantine churches** and the **Archaeological Museum.**

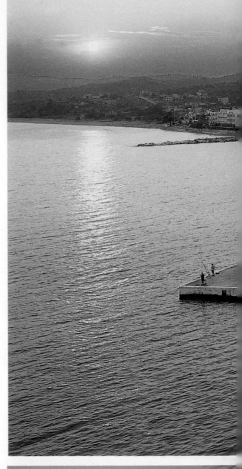

THASOS

A t a distance of 17 nautical miles from Kavala lies the verdant island of Thasos, the only island within Macedonia. Thasos has been inhabited without interruption since the Neolithic period, but it flourished more than ever before in historical times and particularly after its colonisation from Paros in the seventh century BC. In the sixth century BC, it reached the height of its prosperity, thanks to the fertility of its soil, to trade in the renowned wine of the island and to the deposits of silver and gold found in its soil. After the fifth century BC, Thasos belonged successively to Athens, Sparta, Macedon and Rome. These conquerors were followed by the Byzantines, the Venetians and the Turks. Unification with Greece came in 1913. The chief town of the island retains many structures which recall the ancient city, while the local **Archaeological Museum** houses some superb works of art which demonstrate that the city's wealth in antiquity was not just a matter of trade and industry.

pp. 244-245
The only island in Macedonia is densely wooded and has a variety of landscapes to offer: sandy beaches backed by woods on the east side, calm seas to the north and west, and steep rocky shores to the south.

THRACE

T hrace occupies the most north-easterly corner of Greece, bordering on the north with Bulgaria, on the east with Turkey and on the west with the geographical region of Macedonia. To the south, it is washed by the Thracian Sea (the North Aegean), while the rivers Evros (Hebrus) and Nestos mark the eastern and western boundaries of Thrace. The terrain is largely low-lying, and such hills as the area can boast are outrunners of the Rhodope range further to the north. The only lake in Thrace is Lake Vistonis, which is joined to the bay of Porto Lagos through a narrow alluvial channel. Administratively, Thrace is divided into the Prefectures of Xanthi, Rhodope and Evros, and - like Macedonia - it has only one island, Samothrace.

Thrace was first inhabited in the Palaeolithic period, as finds from the plains of the rivers Adras and Evros have shown. Excavations at Stryme, Makri and Paradimi have brought to light traces of important Neolithic settlements, while the villages of the Bronze Age reveal that there were links at that time between Thrace and Lesbos, Lemnos and Troy. The first Indo-European tribes entered Thrace around 2000 BC, and in the eleventh century BC the first Thracian peoples settled in the area. During the seventh century BC, most of the coastal sites were colonised by immigrants from central Greece and the Aegean islands, and some of these colonies grew into important city-states (Abdera, Maronia, Mesembria, and others). Before long,

p. 246-247

Thrace, where east and west meet, is the most unspoiled part of Greece.
The wetland of the Evros estuary is home to more than 300 species of birds, which nest, winter or stay for briefer periods by the river.

p. 248
The archaeological site at Abdera, one of the earliest colonies in Thrace. The site where the colonists from Clazomenae first settled, on the estuary of the river Nestos, has been identified.

the new arrivals managed to impose their rule over the old Thracian tribes, to whom they passed on the culture they brought with them. During the Persian Wars, Thrace was occupied by the Persians. Liberated from them by Athens in 477 BC, it joined the Athenian League and followed the fluctuating fortunes of Athens until the middle of the fourth century BC. In 349 BC, Thrace came under Macedonian control, where it remained until becoming a Roman province in 46 BC. Between the second century AD and conquest by the Franks in 1204, Thrace was subjected to constant raids by the Goths, the Huns and the Bulgars, passing into Turkish hands when Constantinople fell in 1453. During the First Balkan War (1913), Thrace was briefly liberated, but the peace treaties which concluded the Second Balkan War made the eastern half of it over to Turkey. The rest of Thrace was incorporated into Greece in 1923.

ABDERA

Abdera stands on the coast of Thrace, between the mouth of the river Nestos and Lake Vistonis. The city was founded in the sixth century BC by colonists from Clazomenae, but their colony was soon taken over and rebuilt by new arrivals from the city of Teo (544 BC). The city grew steadily until the fourth century BC, with the

exception of the period 482-479 BC, when it was under Persian control. In 376 BC, the tribe called the Triballi sacked Abdera and reduced it to obscurity, while in 343 BC it was taken by the Macedonians and in 170 BC by Rome. Abdera was the birthplace of some of the most important personalities of antiquity, including the philosopher Democritus, the historian Hecataeus and the Sophist Protagoras. Today, traces of the ancient buildings of the city are still to be seen: **houses** and **workshops** of the Hellenistic period, Roman **tombs**, sections of the fourth-century **walls**, of the **acropolis** and of the **ports**, and a **theatre**, probably dating from the Classical period.

KOMOTINI

Komotini is the chief town of the Prefecture of Rhodope and one of the most important commercial and economic centres of Thrace as well as being a major transport junction. The character if the town is of particular interest because of its marked 'Oriental' tone, which is particularly strong in the old quarter. In the centre of the modern town, sections of the **Byzantine fortifications** have survived: there was a way-station on the Via Egnatia here. The **Archaeological Museum** of Komotini, which houses a collection of finds from all over Thrace, is of the greatest interest.

p. 249
Komotini

THE EVROS ESTUARY

The estuary of the river Evros is one of the most important wetlands in Greece and, indeed, in Europe. The amazing landscape is the result of alternating areas of dry land and shallow water, and the ecological significance of the site stems from its wealth of waterfowl and fish. There are numerous endemic species, and the area is used by vast flocks of migrating birds each year. Today, concerted efforts are being made to conserve the ecological balance of this unique area.

SAMOTHRACE

Samothrace is a beautiful mountainous island whose highest peak is Fengari, at 1800 m. on Mt Saos. The earliest proper village on the island, dating from Neolithic times, was at **Mikro Vouni** on the south-west coast. The first Greek colonists were Aeolians from Asia Minor, or possibly Lesbos. The city they founded prospered in the seventh and sixth centuries BC, and later developed into a religious centre for the whole of the Greek world because of its mystic cult of the Great Gods (the Cabeiroi). Excavations have revealed the ruins of the **Sanctuary of the Great Gods**, together with an interesting circular structure dating from the third century BC (the **Arsinoeium**) and parts of the city **walls.** In the archaeological site is a **museum** with finds from all over Samothrace. They include a copy of the famous Nike of Samothrace, the original of which is now in the Louvre. Today, Samothrace with its streams and abundant greenery is an ideal refuge for nature-lovers.

MARONIA

Maronia stands to the south of Komotini, on the site of ancient Ismarus, which was founded in the seventh century BC by colonists from the island of Chios. Thanks to its harbour and its fertile soil, Maronia developed into one of the richest cities in Thrace. In the fifth century BC, Maronia joined the Athenian League and in the fourth century a wall some 10 km. in length was constructed round it. Today, in the pretty village which retains the ancient name, an extensive archaeological site contains traces of a large number of ancient buildings. Architectural members from basilicas of the Early Christian period have also come to light, as have ruins of Byzantine buildings which demonstrate that the city still flourished in later times.

p. 250
Mosaic floor from a house in Maronia; 3rd century BC.

p. 251
Views of Samothrace
The sanctuary of the Great Gods on Samothrace, where mysteries comparable to those of Eleusis were held.

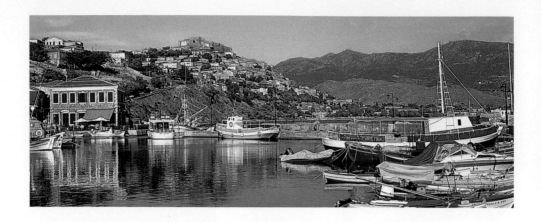

THE ISLANDS OF THE AEGEAN

p. 252
Above: Molyvos, ancient Methymna, one of the prettiest villages on Lesbos.

p. 253
The church of St Therapon in Mytilene.

THE NORTH-EAST AEGEAN

Lemnos - Ayios Efstratios

There is a tradition that the picturesque island of Lemnos is where Hephaestus, the god of metalworkers, had his forge, which explained why the early islanders were famed for their skills as blacksmiths. Later, the Minyans - one of the oldest peoples in mainland Greece - also ruled in Lemnos. Excavations have revealed an important prehistoric setttlement at **Poliochni**, dating back to the fourth millennium BC and reconstructed at least twice. Lemnos, like Samothrace, had a sanctuary to the Cabeiroi, which has been excavated at Ifaisteia. Myrina has an **archaeological museum** with interesting finds from all over the island. Eighteen nautical miles off the coast of Lemnos is the volcanic, sparsely-populated island of **Ayios Efstratios**, which was used as a place of exile in former times.

Lesbos (Lesvos, Mytilene)

Lesbos is the third-largest island in Greece. The first inhabitants seem to have settled in the vicinity of **Thermi** in the fourth millennium BC. In the second

p. 254

View of Myrina on Lemnos. Above the town towers a Venetian castle which occupies the site of ancient Myrina.

Below: Lesbos, view of Molyvos.

millennium BC, the island was taken over successively by Pelasgians, Achaeans and - last of all - Aeolians, who encouraged the growth of trade and founded colonies in Thrace and Asia Minor. In the seventh and sixth centuries BC, Lesbos was the birthplace of many important personalities, including the poets Alcaeus, Terpander, Arion and Sappho, who between them founded Greek lyric poetry, and Pittacus, one of the Seven Sages of antiquity. After a brief spell of Persian Rule (492-479 BC), Lesbos joined the Athenian League; seceding from this in 428 BC, the island was punished by being divided into holdings of land distributed among Athenian citizens. In 88 BC, Lesbos came under Roman control, and from that point on was an ordinary Roman - and later Byzantine - province. In 1355, the Genoese prince Francesco Gatelluso received the island as part of his wife's

dowry, and his dynasty turned it into one of the most important administrative and commercial centres of the north Aegean. In 1462, Lesbos fell to the Turks, remaining in their hands until liberation in 1912. Lesbos is a verdant island with a wide range of features of interest to visitors. The principal sights in the chief town, Mytilene (by which name the whole island is also sometimes known), are the **medieval castle**, the nineteenth century **mansions**, the interesting **archaeological museum** and, at Vareia, the **museum** dedicated to the work of the naif painter **Theophilos**. There are fascinating fishing-villages to be seen all over the island. **Molyvos** has a castle built by the Gatellusi, **Ayiasos** has a famous church of Our Lady, and at **Sigri** there is a petrified forest dating back millions of years.

p. 255

Plomari, the second-largest town on Lesvos, is a centre for trade and shipping.

Chios - Oinouses - Psara

Chios is a rocky island to the south of Mytilene; in antiquity, it was called Macris and Ophiousa. The first inhabitants were Leleges and Pelasgians, while in the historical period it was colonised by Ionians from Attica. In Classical times, it underwent a short period of Persian occupation (499-472 BC) before joining the Athenian League and ultimately attaining independence in 355 BC. The island then passed to the Macedonians (331 BC) and later the Romans (84 BC). Between the seventh and the eleventh century AD it suffered much at the hands of Saracen pirates. At this time, the town of Chios was fortified with strong walls, and the monuments built included the very important **Nea Moni** ('new monastery'). The *katholikon* of the foundation (1043-1055) was built at the expense of the Emperor Constantine Monomachus, in the octagonal architectural type, and ornamented with superb mosaics. In 1346, Chios came under the control of Genoese princes, remaining in their hands until 1566, when it was captured by the Turks. It is to the Genoese period that the **Mastichochoria** can trace their origins: located in the south of the island, the economy of these villages is

p. 256
Life in the smaller islands of the Aegean rolls quietly along, without disturbance from the few tourists.

based on the production of mastic, a substance which even today is exclusive to Chios. Life continues largely unchanged in these medieval walled villages, giving the visitor a unique opportunity to see a type of architecture which elsewhere has largely vanished. The villages where mastic was produced received privileges from the Turks which allowed them to develop trade and industry. Chios was liberated in 1912.

Oinouses is actually a group of tiny islands off the north-east coast of Chios. Only one of the islands is inhabited, and it is an ideal place for quiet holidays. On Oinouses is a **Maritime Museum** which gives a fascinating picture of the seafaring tradition of the island.

Psara lies to the north-west of Chios, and has gone down in history principally on account of the fate of its inhabitants during the Greek War of Independence. The commercial fleet of Psara was the third-largest in all Greece, and it held out for months against the numerically superior Turkish forces. But in June 1824, the Greeks were forced to surrender, and the island of Psara was utterly devastated by the vengeful Turks. The destruction of the island shocked the whole of Europe, and provided a theme for many artists of the time. Today, there is only one small village on Psara, and tourism is restricted.

p. 257
Views of Chios.

Ikaria - Fourni

It was close to Ikaria, according to the myths, that Icarus plunged into the sea and was killed when his flight too close to the sun caused the wax on the wings made by his father Daedalus to melt. The island was colonised from Miletus in the eighth century BC. In the early fifth century BC, it came under Persian rule, and not long afterwards joined the Athenian League. By the first century AD, however, the island was deserted, and in the Byzantine era it was a place of exile. Ikaria was annexed to Greece in 1912. Today, it is known for its hot medicinal baths, which have been famous since ancient times.

Very close to Ikaria is the group of tiny, sparsely-populated islands called **Fourni**, a paradise for modern explorers off the beaten track.

Samos

The green island of Samos has always, throughout its long history, been at the centre of artistic and cultural developments in Greece. The first inhabitants seem to have settled on the island in the fourth millennium BC, in the area where the chief town of Samos was later founded. The Greek tribes overran the island in the second millenium BC, and the first Ionian colonists arrived around 900 BC; it was to them that the island owed its development at an early stage in its history. In the eighth or seventh century BC, the first **temple of Hera** was built: Hera was the predominant deity on Samos, and had been worshipped at a distinct shrine since the tenth century BC. More temples were built in her honour down to the sixth century BC, the most important of them being that constructed by Polycrates in 525 BC, which is the largest temple in Greece. Polycrates was tyrant of Samos, and ruled from 532 to 522 BC. A number of huge public works projects were constructed during his reign, and the island prospered. It was at this time that the great philosopher and mathematician Pythagoras was born on Samos. After the fifth century BC, Samos passed successively through the hands of Athens, Sparta, Macedon and Rome. In the Byzantine period, it was raided by the Goths, the Huns, the Alans and Saracen pirates before coming under the control of the Genoese and other Westerners. After 1453, the island was deserted, and recolonisation did not begin until 1562 - when, of course, it was under Turkish rule. In 1832, Samos was declared autonomous, and in 1912 it was unified with Greece.

p. 258
Only one column of the Ionic temple of Hera on Samos still stands. The work of the tyrant Polycrates (525 BC), this was the largest ancient temple in Greece, measuring 55 by 112 metres.

p. 259
Above: view of Pythagorio, the busiest tourist resort on Samos.

Below: Tsamadou beach, backed by dense greenery as are most of the beaches on Samos. In the background, the village of Kokkari, one of the island's prettiest.

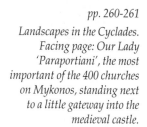

pp. 260-261
Landscapes in the Cyclades.
Facing page: Our Lady
'Paraportiani', the most
important of the 400 churches
on Mykonos, standing next
to a little gateway into the
medieval castle.

THE CYCLADES

The Cyclades are a group of islands in the Aegean which are in effect the mountain peaks of the sunken continent of Aegeis. They consist of two approximately parallel lines of islands (Andros, Tinos, Mykonos, Delos and Rhenia; Kea, Kythnos, Serifos and Sifnos) at the centre of which lie Syros and Yaros, with a third line across the southern extremity of the first two (Naxos, Paros and Antiparos). The islands of Milos, Folegandros, Kimolos, Sikinos, Ios, Amorgos, Anafi, Thira (Santorini) and Makronisos also belong, administratively, to the Cyclades. The name 'Cyclades' dates back to ancient times, and stems from the fact that all the islands form a kind of circle around Delos, the sacred island of the ancient Greeks. The Cyclades are mountainous, barren islands, but their unique architectural character has contributed much to the image which most foreigners have of Greece. The low, whitewashed houses with their courtyards full of fragrant flowers, the narrow cobbled lanes, the bare mountains leading down to sandy beaches, the calm sea and the hot summer sun - these are the components of a dream which leaves none of the world's travellers unaffected.

As a result of their geographical position, the Cyclades have long been a bridge between East and West, and they have played an important part in the history of the Greek world. Traces of habitation in the Neolithic period have come to light on Kea, Naxos and

p. 262

Above: the Lion Terrace on Delos. The superb lion statues protected the sacred lake at the sanctuary of Leto.

Below: Naxos, the monumental doorway of the Ionic temple of Apollo, built in 530 BC by the tyrant Lygdamis.

Antiparos (Salangos), and in the Early Bronze Age a unique civilisation - today called 'Cycladic' - formed in the islands (3rd millennium BC). Our knowledge of the Cycladic civilisation stems from the numerous sites which archaeologists have discovered in the islands. In those early times, the islanders were farmers, shepherds, fishermen or merchants trading in the valuable goods of the age: obsidian from Milos, copper from Serifos and Sifnos, marble from Paros and Naxos. The islanders of the Cyclades were

skilled in the arts and crafts, and particularly in pottery, sculpture and metal-working. The most representative examples of Cycladic art are the marble statuettes found in the area, and now to be seen in most Greek museums and in many collections in other countries. The statuettes depict nude female figures, usually upright but occasionally seated, which impress the viewer with their abstractive, plain and severe proportions. These features remained consistent throughout the Bronze Age, but in the later subdivi-

sions of the period there are clear influences from Minoan Crete, which had begun to penetrate and dominate the Aegean. The most important settlement of the Late Bronze Age was found at Akrotiri on Thera. In the historical period, most of the Cycladic islands were colonised by Ionians, although some of them - such as Thera and Milos - were Doric colonies. After the late ninth century BC, Delos, the island where Apollo was born, became a fully-fledged sanctuary to the god and evolved into a religious centre of importance for the entire Greek world. The growth of shipping and trade as early as the Archaic period, and contacts with lands further to the east through the various colonies, fostered the development of the Cyclades. In the seventh century BC, and particularly in the sixth, Cycladic art made important steps forward under the influence of nearby Ionia. In the early fifth century, the islands came under Persian control, and were liberated after 480 BC, when they joined the Athenian League. When the Pelopon-

p. 263
View of Oia, the prettiest village on Santorini, is a unique sight with its brilliantly-white houses set against the steep volcanic cliffs.

nesian War was over, Sparta became the dominant power, and it was not until 375 BC that the Cyclades came back into the Athenian sphere of influence. In 363 BC they were occupied by Epaminondas of Thebes for a short period, and in 338 BC the Macedonians took over. Under the Romans, the islands suffered at the hands of various barbarians, and in Byzantine times they underwent the depredations of the Slavs and the Saracens. After 1204, they were occupied by Franks, Venetians and Turks.

Although there is a general uniformity about the Cyclades today, each island has its own distinctive personality, and each has something unique to offer the visitor.

On **Kea** (or **Tzia**), we can visit the prehistoric settlement at **Ayia Irini** and the **archaeological museum** in Ioulida, chief town of the island.

Kythnos is known for its hot medicinal springs at Loutra and is also an ideal place for quiet holidays - as is **Serifos**, whose chief town has a ruined Venetian castle.

On **Sifnos**, the chief town (**Apollonia**) is built on an impressive, naturally amphitheatrical site. There are many monasteries, including those of the **Prophet Elijah** (8th century) and **Our Lady 'Chrysopigi'** (17th century), and some most attractive villages.

Volcanic **Milos** is still rich in mineral deposits even today. In prehistoric times, it was the only place in the Greek world where obsidian was mined and exported. Near the villlage of Apollonia are the remains of the prehistoric settlement of **Phylacope**. The village of Klima was the location where the famous statue of the **Venus di Milo**, now in the Louvre, was discovered. Klima also preserves some superb **catacombs** dating from the Early Christian period.

The islands of **Kimolos, Folegandros** and **Sikinos** are tiny, half-forgotten paradises - while **Ios**, by way of contrast, is a tourist resort of considerable importance. Above the chief town of Ios stand the remains of a Venetian castle, occupying the ancient Acropolis, with a line of the windmills so typical of the Cyclades stretching further to the north.

Thira (Santorini) is a unique sight, with its cliffs towering out of the sea and the volcanic crater in which are the islets of **Thirasia, Aspronisi,** and **Nea** and **Palaia Kammeni**. The chief town, **Fira**, clings to the lip of the crater, and is one of the most cosmopolitan places anywhere in the Mediterranean. On the hill called Profitis Ilias are the ruins of **the ancient city of Thera** (the agora, the theatre, and many public and private buildings). Of particular interest is the traditional architecture of Fira and also of **Oia**, in the north of the island. To the south are the ruins of the prehistoric settlement at **Akrotiri**, finds from which are to be seen in the old and new **museums** at Fira. This is the

best-preserved prehistoric settlement to have come to light anywhere in the Aegean. The buildings have survived in good condition because the eruption of the volcano of Thera, in about 1500 BC, covered them with a thick layer of volcanic ash, keeping the ruins safe down the centuries. The Akrotiri settlement flourished in 1550-1500 BC, and can be seen to have reached an advanced cultural level as it assimilated what the Minoans of Crete could offer it. The famous wall-paintings which ornamented many of the buildings of the settlement are of unique artistic and archaeological value. Very close to Santorini is **Anafi**, a small but idyllic island, and further to the north is **Amorgos**, one of the most typical of the Cycladic islands. Amorgos has the ruins of three ancient cities (Aegiale, Arcesine, Minoa), as well as an impressive Venetian **castle** in the chief town and the monastery of **Chozoviotissa** (11th century), hewn out of the rock.

Naxos is the largest and most fertile of the Cyclades. It has a wealth of history behind it, and many important ancient sites can be seen there today. Prehistoric settlements, most of them dating from the third millenium BC, have come to light at various points on the island. At **Grotta**, in the chief town of Naxos, there are indications of habitation from the Neolithic period down to Mycenean times, while sections of the Mycenean wall have been discovered close to the **Cathedral** of Naxos. The most impressive monument of all, of course, is the huge gateway to the Ionic temple of Apollo at **Palatia** (530 BC). The area around the **Venetian castle** of Naxos town is particularly picturesque. The old French College,

p. 266

Views of Santorini. In very early times, the island was called Strongyle; when the volcano erupted around 1500 BC, part of the island sank beneath the waves and Santorini took its current form.

p. 267

Above: wall-paintings from the site at Akrotiri, Santorini: the Boxers, the Fisherman, the Spring Fresco (1550-1500 BC, National Archaeological Museum, Athens).

Below: view of Oia, the prettiest village on Santorini, with distinctive local architecture.

a building dating from 1637, houses the **archaeological museum** of Naxos, which provides the visitor with a good overview of Cycladic art. The **archaeological museum** at Apeiranthos is of almost equal importance. A sumptuous shrine to Demeter and Kore (the **Telesterium**, 530 BC) has been excavated at the village of Sangri and a sanctuary of **Dionysus** has come to light at Iria, while Apollonas and Melanes have yielded two important **ancient quarries** and three half-finished Archaic *kouroi* of enormous dimensions. Naxos also has a large number of well-preserved **Byzantine churches**, many of them ornamented with outstanding wall-paintings: Our Lady 'Protothroni' at Chalki, St John the Divine, Our Lady 'Drosiani', St Kyriake, St Artemius, St George 'Diasoritis', St Nicholas at Sangri, and others.

Paros, too, is of archaeological interest. The chief town, **Parikia**, has yielded traces of a Cycladic settlement, in the area occupied by the ancient acropolis. In the vicinity there was also a **temple of Athena** (530-520 BC), while to the north of the town were shrines to **Apollo Delius** and **Artemis**, with a sanctuary of **Pythian Apollo** to the south west. Athena was also worshipped at the spot known as **Koukounaries**, near Naousa, and the goddess's temple, built around 700 BC, has been discovered. In prehistoric times, there was an important settlement founded in the thirteenth or twelfth century BC at Koukounaries,

p. 268
View of Ios.

p. 269
Above: Naousa, Paros, a pretty and bustling village with a ruined Venetian castle.

Below: Little Venice in the main town of Mykonos.

Launches carry visitors back and forth from Mykonos to **Delos**, which is uninhabited today but where there is a vast archaeological site with the remains of the **sanctuary of Apollo**. According to the myths, it was in the shade of a tree on Delos that Leto gave birth to Apollo and Artemis, and it was from this dual divine birth that the island acquired its sanctity. In 478 BC it became the centre of the Athenian (or Delian) League. In 426 BC, the Athenians ordered the purification of Delos, with the removal to the nearby islet of **Rhenia** of the bones of all those who had ever died on Delos. After that time, both births and deaths were forbidden on the sacred island. The most important of the ruins to be seen today are those of the **Agora**, the numerous **stoas**, the **Propylaea, the house of the Naxians, the Sacred Way, the temples of Apollo, Treasuries, the Prytanaeum, the Artemisium, the Agora of the Italians, the Hippodrome, the Stadium, the Agora of the Delians, the Aphrodisium, the Heraeum, the Theatre** and a whole host of **houses** of the Hellenistic and Roman periods, ornamented with superb mosaics. In the archaeological site is a **museum** with finds from the area.

and the finds from it are on display in the **archaeological museum** of Parikia, along with a collection of items from all over the island. Other points of interest in Parikia include the **medieval castle**, constructed out of ancient building materials, and the church of **Our Lady 'Katapoliani'**, founded by Constantine the Great and altered in the time of Justinian.

Very close to Paros is **Antiparos**: the two islands were one in prehistoric times. The islet of **Salangos**, between Paros and Antiparos, has yielded the remains of an important Neolithic settlement.

Mykonos is the Cycladic island *par excellence*, and it is extremely popular as a tourist destination. The chief town, with its crown of quaint windmills, is a very cosmopolitan place today. Overlooking the harbour is the church of **Paraportiani**, the most important of the 400 or so churches which the island can boast. The collection of the **archaeological museum** consists largely of finds from the necropolis of Rhenia (see below). There are also interesting exhibits in the **Folklore** and **Nautical** Museums of Mykonos.

The pretty island of **Syros** is the capital of all the Cyclades. **Ermoupoli**, chief town of the island, stands on a naturally amphitheatrical site between two hills and preserves many fine neo-Classical buildings to remind the visitor of the time when this was a flourishing centre of shipping and industry. The most impressive neo-Classical structures are those of the **Town Hall** (designed by Ernst Ziller), the **Apollo Theatre** (a

p. 270
Mosaic of dolphins from the House of the Dolphins, Delos.

replica in miniature of La Scala in Milan), and the **Cathedral** (1842). In the **archaeological museum** are finds from all over the island. A fortified settlement of the third millennium BC has come to light at **Halandriani** on Syros (Kastri) and seems to have been an important centre for the Cycladic civilisation.

Tinos is most famous for its church of **Our Lady of the Annunciation**, founded in 1823 to house the miraculous icon of Our Lady and today the destination of a pilgrimage which attracts the faithful from all over Greece. The islanders of Tinos are also known for their achievements in marble sculpture, while there are **dovecotes** to be seen all over

the island. In the chief town of the island is a **museum of modern art**, with an interesting **archaeological museum.**

Andros was once called 'Hydrousa', the island of water, because of its medicinal springs. The chief town stands on the site of a medieval city and preserves the remains of a **Venetian castle**. Ruins of ancient Andros have come to light at the village of Palaiopoli.

The finds from this site are housed in an ultra-modern **archaeological museum** in the chief town. The **museum of modern art**, where exhibitions are held during the summer months, is another cultural facility of great interest.

p. 271

Chora, Mykonos, and its bustling harbour. In the background a line of the windmills characteristic of the landscape.

p. 272
Above: Mandraki harbour in Rhodes town, with the three surviving medieval mills.

Below: marble head of the god Helios (second century BC, Rhodes Archaeological Museum).

THE DODECANESE

The group of islands called the Dodecanese lie in the eastern Aegean, being bounded on the east by the coast of Asia Minor, on the west by the Cyclades, on the north by Samos and Ikaria and on the south by Crete. Although the name means 'twelve islands', the group actually consists of 14 islands and some 80 rocky islets, most of them uninhabited. The most important islands are Patmos, Leros, Kalymnos, Kos, Nisyros, Astypalaia, Tilos, Syme, Chalki, Rhodes, Kastellorizo, Karpathos and Kasos.

Thanks to their position close to Asia and in the direction of Africa, the Dodecanese have often been the target of marauders, and their history has been a troubled one. In the fifteenth century BC, the first Achaean settlers arrived, probably from Crete, though they were later driven out by Dorian invaders. The Dorians fostered the development of the islands, which by the seventh century BC had founded colonies to the east and west. In the Persian Wars, most of the Dodecanese islands came under Persian control, and fought on their side against the other Greeks. After the Greek victory at the battle of Salamis in 480 BC, however, the islanders were able to shake off the Persian yoke. After this time, each island followed its own course through history down to the Middle Ages. The Dodecanese played an important part in the history of the Crusades, since many of the island harbours were used

◄ p. 273
Above: the acropolis of Lindos, Rhodes, with the ruins of a temple of Athena.

p. 274
Above: view of Kos.

Below: columns from the Doric temple of Apollo on the ancient acropolis of Rhodes.

as operational bases. After 1204, the islands formed an independent state, with Leo Gavalas as its prince, and in 1250 they were ruled directly by the Emperor of Nicaea, which was the rump Byzantine state. In 1303, Kasos and Karpathos were taken by Andreas Cornaros of Crete, and in 1306 Rhodes, Kos and Leros were sold to the Knights Templar of St John, whose realm ultimately extended to include Chalki, Syme, Tilos and Kalymnos as

well. In 1522, the Turks drove out the Knights of St John and established themselves, granting the islands many privileges and a considerable degree of autonomy. In 1912 the Dodecanese islands were occupied by Italy, not being finally annexed to Greece until 1946-1948.

The most northerly of the Dodecanese is **Patmos**, the holy island of the Revelation. It was there that St John the Divine composed his

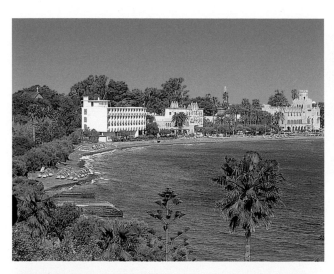

prophetic book, in a cave which can still be seen today. Above the chief town of Patmos towers the **monastery of St John the Divine**, fortified by a strong wall. It was founded in 1088 and is one of the most important treasures of Byzantine art, with superb wall-paintings, icons, ecclesiastical relics and a library with important manuscripts and codices.

Leros is an attractive and fertile island which is ideal for quiet holidays.

Kalymnos, the island of sponge-fishers, is mountainous and rocky and can boast only one stretch of flat land, though this is very fertile.

Kos, the island where the great physician Hippocrates was born in the fifth century BC, combines natural beauty with numerous important ancient monuments. In the chief town are remains of the ancient city: **the port, the agora, the sanctuary of Aphrodite Pandemos** (2nd century

p. 275
View of Chora, Patmos. Above the town rises the fortified Monastery of St John the Divine, close to which is the cave in which the saint, in exile, wrote the Book of Revelation.

BC), **the stadium, Roman baths, stoas, a gymnasium** (2nd century BC), Hellenistic and Roman **houses** with fine mosaic ornamentation, and the superb **Casa Romana**, now restored, dating from the second century BC. Also to be seen is the **castle** of the Knights of St John, where there is an open-air museum. Of particular interest is the **archaeological museum** of Kos, which has an excellent collection of sculptures, most of them dating from the Hellenistic and Roman periods. Very close to the main town is the archaeological site of the **Asclepium** of Kos (Hellenistic period), with the ruins of the most important centre for early Greek medicine.

The volcanic island of **Nisyros** is a place of unique beauty. In the centre of the island is a volcanic crater with a diameter of 4 km. **Astypalaia**, too, is of volcanic origin, consisting of two pieces of land joined by a narrow isthmus. The deeply-indented shoreline means that there are plenty of idyllic bays for swimming. Above the natural amphitheatre which is the site of the island's chief town towers a thirteenth century **Venetian castle**.

Tilos, sparsely-populated and off the tourist trail, is a tiny paradise of dense vegetation and plentiful streams.

Syme is a barren island close to the shore of Asia Minor. The chief town is crowned with the castle dating from the time of the Knights of St John, and is notable for its many neo-Classical houses. There are Byzantine churches all over the island, whose patron saint is St Michael: his church (18th century) at **Panormitis Bay** attracts many pilgrims to the island.

Chalki is the smallest inhabited

p. 276

Above: the Corinthian columns of the temple of Apollo in the Asklepeiun, Kos.

Below: Chora, Nisyros - an ideal island for quiet holidays.

p. 277

Above: Kos harbour. On the south-east side is the Castello, built in the late fourteenth century by the Knights of St John.

Below: Chora, Astypalaia, on the side of a hill crowned with a thirteenth-century Venetian castle.

p. 278
Views of the Palace of the Grand Master, Rhodes.

island in the Dodecanese, but even so the terrain of the island is highly varied. In antiquity, it was known for its copper mines, to which it owes its name ('chalkos' = copper). Among the picturesque houses of the chief town stands the church of **St Nicholas**, with its bell-tower, while above Chora, the old capital, a **medieval castle** stands atop a steep cliff.

The most important and largest of the Dodecanese islands is **Rhodes**, which thanks to its great natural beauty and the wealth of its historical past has been highly developed for tourism. Rhodes is among the most cosmopolitan islands in the Mediterranean. The three ancient cities of the island are of great archaeological interest. **Lindos**, where today there is an attractive village and a fine beach, preserves ruins of the Hellenistic san-

ctuary and temple of Athena Lindia (c. 330 BC). The acropolis of ancient **Ialysos** has come to light on **Mt Phile-rimos**, with traces of a prehistoric settlement in the immediate vicinity. The third of the Doric cities of Rhodes was **Kameiros**, where a temple of Athena has been discovered together with numerous houses. In 408 BC, these cities united to found a new capital on the north side of the island: Rhodes itself.

Most of the surviving traces of ancient Rhodes are to be seen on **Monte Smith hill** (the acropolis, the theatre, the stadium, the temples of Apollo and Athena). The picturesque **old town** of Rhodes, on the other hand, reflects the medieval history of the island. The entire town is surrounded by impressive **walls** dating from the time of the Knights of St John, while within it, restored by the Italians, are many build-

p. 279

Rhodes.

In front of the Palace of the Grand Master is the New Market, and part of the harbour can be seen.

p. 280
Above: view of Karpathos.
Below: Chora, Symi, with neo-Classical houses stretching up the sides of a hill crowned with a castle built by the Knights of St John.

ings of the same period and the imposing **Palace of the Grand Master**. The port of Rhodes (**Mandraki**), straddled according to tradition by the famous bronze statue of the Colossus, is a place of unique interest, with the Tower of St Nicholas, the old windmills and the statues of two deer on high pillars along its seafront. Interesting buildings from the period of Italian rule are to be seen in the area around Mandraki, while the monuments of the Byzantine and Turkish periods give the old town an atmos-

phere all its own. The entire past of Rhodes and the history of its achievements in the arts (with the main emphasis on the Hellenistic period) is to be seen in the **archaeological museum**, housed in the Hospital of the Knights. The modern city has tourist amenities of all kinds, and the island of Rhodes is packed with sites and places of great beauty and interest.

To the east of Rhodes lies **Kastellorizo**, an idyllic spot which is ideal for quiet holidays. Excavations on the island have brought to light the ruins of

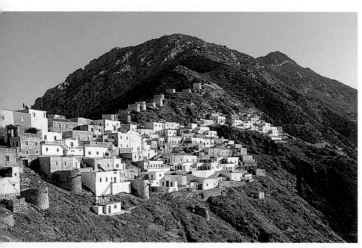

a Mycenean settlement, and the numerous finds dating from the historic period are housed in a small **archaeological museum**. The chief town is lent added picturesqueness by its whitewashed houses, whose multicoloured doors and windows are reflected in the waters of the harbour.

Although **Karpathos** is large in terms of size, it is barren, isolated and depopulated. This is perhaps why some very old traditions have managed to survive down to the present day. In the village of **Olympos**, for ex-ample, the local people use a dialect in which there are traces of the Doric tongue. Karpathos has the remains of three ancient cities, and at **Pigadi** (ancient Poseidio) there is a private collection whose finds cover the period from the Mycenean period down to Hellenistic times.

Kasos, the most southerly island in the Dodecanese, is not often visited by tourists. It is a mountainous island, with a rocky coast, and the few beaches are close to the main town (**Fri**) and the port of **Emborio**.

p. 281

Left: Chora, Kastellorizo.

Right: scenes from Karpathos, a living museum thanks to the unspoiled traditions and linguistic individualities of the local people.

CRETE

Crete, a place of unique beauty, is the largest Greek island and the fifth-largest in the Mediterranean. It forms the southernmost extremity of Greece, and constitutes a bridge for communications between Europe and Africa.

According to the myths, Crete was the birthplace of Zeus, the *primus inter pares* of the Olympian gods. By Europa, Zeus fathered Minos, the mythical king of the island, who in turn gave his name to the Minoan civilisation, the oldest on the European continent. In the palace of Minos, known as the Labyrinth and designed by the architect Daedalus, lived the Minotaur, a monster with the body of a man and the head of a bull. The Minotaur is connected with the myth of the Athenian hero Theseus, who succeeded in killing the monster with the help of Ariadne, daughter of Minos. Thus he released the Athenians from the tribute of blood (seven youths and seven maidens, fed to the Minotaur) which the city had been obliged to pay to Minos.

These myths tell us much about the power which Crete had acquired in prehistoric times, as also confirmed beyond any doubt by archaeological finds.

Crete was first inhabited in the Neolithic era, but the most brilliant period in its history was the Bronze Age. Archaeologists distinguish four phases in Minoan history, in line with the founding and destruction of the Minoan palaces.

In the Pre-Palace period (2600-2000 BC), the island escaped from the isolation of the Neolithic era and began to develop in every possible way, heralding the progress to be made in later centuries. It was at this time that the Minoans adopted a hieroglyphic script.

In the Early Palace period (2000-1700 BC), the first Minoan **palaces** were built at Knossos, Phaestos, Malia and Zakro. These were labyrinthine structures around which the entire settlement was organised and in which all its wealth was kept. The religious needs of the Cretans were served by **shrines** on the peaks of mountains. A vast quantity of finds from this period has come to light, and they impress us with the skill and delicacy of their manufacture.

In 1700 BC, a severe earthquake badly damaged the island, but in the Late Palace period (1700-1450 BC), new and equally magnificent palaces were built at **Knossos, Phaestos, Malia, Zakro** and **Kydonia (Chania)**. These luxurious royal palaces contained the apartments of the king (with wall-paintings), shrines, 'washing tanks' for use during rites of purification, theatrical structures from which the various rituals could be watched, numerous storerooms and workshops, archive rooms, baths, paved courtyards, monumental gateways, staircases to the upper floors and complex arrangements of corridors. The palace at Knossos, much of which has been reconstructed, gives a clear picture of Minoan architecture and occupies an area of 22,000 square metres. During this period, many fascinating **country houses** were built, and examples have been discovered at **Ano Zakro**, **Nirou Hani, Amnisos, Tilisos, Archanes, Ayia Triada** and elsewhere. A clear picture of the tightly-organised Late Palace-period

◄ *p. 282*
Above: the Blue Ladies, a wall-painting from Knossos (1600 BC, Herakleio Arch. Museum).

Below: the snake goddess, a faience statuette from Knossos (1600-1500 BC, Herakleio Arch. Museum).

◄ *p. 283*
Knossos: the north side of the main palace courtyard.

settlements is to be gained from the finds yielded by the sites at **Zakro, Palaikastro, Petra (Siteia), Gournia** and on the islet of **Pseira.** In the Late Palace period, Crete reached the height of its power, dominating the entire Mediterranean (the Minoan thalassocracy). This development is plain in the art of the Minoans, which is best seen in the **archaeological museum of Herakleio**, one of the finest collections in Greece. There are also **museums** at Chania, Rethymno, Archanes, Ayios Nikolaos, Ierapetra and Siteia. Minoan art is notable for a powerful naturalist

spirit, for its free use of colour and for its emphasis on scenes from ordinary life and religious ceremonies.

The wall-paintings found in the palaces and villas are outstanding examples of the artistic concerns of the age. In the Late Palace period, the Minoans used Linear A script, which has not yet been deciphered.

Around 1450 BC, most of the palaces were destroyed, in circumstances of which we do not know the details, while in 1400-1375 BC the palace of Knossos was burned down. In the next period of Cretan history

(the Post-Palace period, 1400-1100 BC), the Myceneans of mainland Greece dominated the island, but they in turn came under the influence of Minoan culture.

The Geometric period saw the emergence of the city-states of Doric Crete (**Aptera, Eleftheria, Gortyna, Phaestos, Knossos, Driros, Lato, Itanos, Siteia** and others), which followed the model of the Spartan system of government. In 69 BC the island was occupied by Rome, inaugurating a period of peace and prosperity. In the second century AD, the Emperor

p. 285

Rethymno harbour and part of the old town, with numerous Venetian and Turkish buildings.

Hadrian demonstrated his fondness for the island by causing magnificent buildings to be constructed in the chief towns. In 824, the Saracens detached the island from the Byzantine Empire, but Nicephorus Phocas liberated it in 961. After 1204, Crete was sold to the Venetians, and the Turks captured it in 1669. In 1898 the island declared its independence, and in 1913 it was united with Greece. During the Second World War, the **battle of Crete** took place on the island, which was a centre for resistance against the occupying forces.

Crete today is one of the most highly-developed tourist resorts in Greece, as a result not only of its wealth of history but also of its natural beauties and the individual features of the daily life and customs of its people. Apart from important archaeological sites and museums, the visitor today can also enjoy places of unique natural beauty (the Samaria Gorge, Frangokastello, Mt Psiloritis, the Kourtaliotiko Gorge, Preveli monastery, Mt Dikte, Matala, the palm forest at Vai, the Lasithi plateau), the picturesque mountain and coastal villages of Crete, some superb caves (Falassarna, Yerani, Melidoni, the Idaean Cave, Zoniana, Trapeza, the Diktaean Cave), historic monasteries (Tzangarola Monastery, Gonia Monastery, Preveli Monastery, Arkadi Monastery, Our Lady 'Kera', Toplou Monastery), and large towns (Chania, Rethymno, Herakleio, Ayios Nikolaos, Siteia), which themselves have plenty of sights and provide a picture of the island's history. Nor does Crete lack idyllic beaches, clear blue seas and isolated, deserted areas which somehow manage to fit in successfully with the ultra-modern tourist infrastructure of the island.

p. 288

From top to bottom: Arkadi Monastery, a typical Cretan beach, windmills on the Lasithi plateau, and Frangokastello.

p. 289

Above: view of Chania harbour.

Below: the world-famous beach at Matala.